ScholarSkills Word-Builders Book 2

Advanced word-building with Latin and Greek roots, prefixes, and suffixes

**Please feel free to forward any questions or comments to info@scholarskillsforstars.com
Your feedback would be greatly appreciated.**

Hints: P-Purple Cards, Y-Yellow Cards, B-Blue Cards, R-Red Cards, G-Green Cards, W-White Cards

Dedication

This book is dedicated to my family and all of the students who are my co-laborers in the quest for excellence.

Introduction:

Vocabulary is the key to success on the Verbal Reasoning and Critical Reading sections of every standardized test. If you are taking the SAT, GRE, ISEE, SHSAT, ELA or any other standardized test, you need to have a rich and varied vocabulary. You need to learn many words--and chances are that you need to learn those words quickly in an easy, effective manner that doesn't overload your already "too busy" schedule. You need to learn more to score more in less time. Word Parts for Word Smarts is a simple way to learn thousands of complex words--fast!

Experts would agree (and the evidence is incontrovertible) that the fastest--and most effective--way to acquire a powerful vocabulary is by learning and applying word parts such as roots, prefixes, and suffixes. Word parts are the building blocks of words, and because English was built primarily on Latin and Greek foundations, hundreds of thousands of words in our language were constructed with Latin and Greek word parts. What's shocking (and really good news for us all) is that most of the Latin and Greek derivatives come from just a few word parts. For example, five prefixes (Im, In, Dis, Re, Un) constitute nearly 57% of all English words with a prefix. It means, also, that the same Latin and Greek elements were used to create thousands of different words.

Directions:

This book will show you how to use the most important word parts to decode complex words. Simply complete the blanks in each section, and keep a list of word parts and derivatives on index cards and you will be well on your way to enriching your vocabulary.

Each of the words has been chosen because it is a “word-multiplier.” This means that each word contains important word parts which enable you to decode many more words. You will also notice that next to each word there are letters with numbers in parentheses, (Y12, R 7) for example. These letters and numbers represent the color-coded word builders that were used to create the words that you are studying. You can use them as flash cards and word-builders that can be used to create words.

To Your Success,

Mr. Vieira

Hints: P-Purple Cards,Y-Yellow Cards, B-Blue Cards, R-Red Cards, G-Green Cards, W-White Cards

Table of Contents:

How to Use This Book:

You are now about to begin the first section where you will use word-parts and context clues to decode definitions. This section contains 100 exercises.

Answers to each of these exercises are found on Word List One in the Appendix that follows this first section.

Finally, we have included a comprehensive list of the most prolific prefixes, roots, and suffixes. This list can be an invaluable guide as you seek to decode new words.

How to complete the exercises:

Step 1:
Read each sentence carefully. Try to ascertain the meaning of the word from the context of the sentence.

Step 2:
Use the code to build the word from its parts. (Example: G5, Y23 means that this word consists of the word-part printed on the Green word-builders card number 5, which is "theo" and the word-part printed on the Yellow word-builders card number 23, which is "cracy." Pay careful attention to the meaning of each word-part.

Step 3:
Write the parts in the designated boxes and place the meaning of each part directly under that part in the box: Write "theo" in the first box and "cracy" in the next box. Write (god) under "theo," and write "rule" under "cracy." Together, these parts create the word "theocracy."

Step 4:
Now try to write the word's meaning based on the sentence and the meaning of its parts. Check the word's meaning in the glossary, which is in Word List One on page 62.

Example:
1. Iran is ruled by a **theocracy**: laws are made by its religious leaders.

***How does this word get its meaning from its parts?* (G5, Y23)**

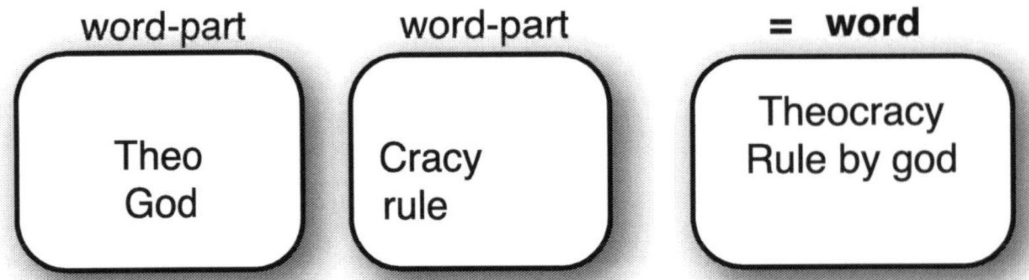

Considering the sentence context and these word-parts, what do you think this word means?

I think that this word means *a nation that is ruled by religion.*

____.

Next, see how close you are to its meaning by consulting the list of definitions.

2. Olympic officials rely on the finest **chronometers** for accuracy during the games. Mistakes in measurement can be disastrous, especially in close races.

***How does this word get its meaning from its parts?* (Y17, R17)**

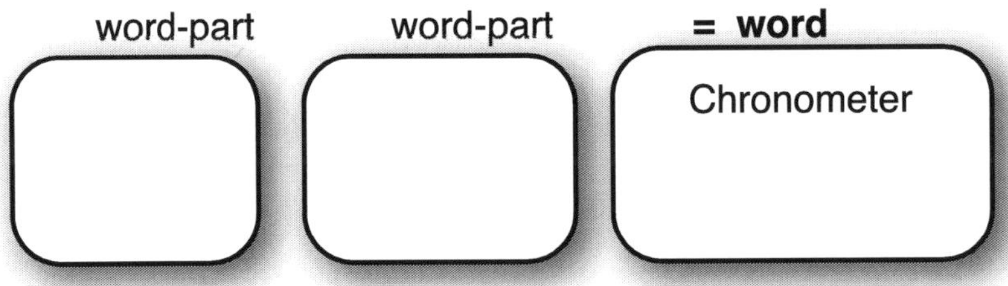

Considering the sentence context and these word-parts, what do you think this word means?
I think that this word means ____

____.

Next, see how close you are to its meaning by consulting the list of definitions.

Hints: P-Purple Cards,Y-Yellow Cards, B-Blue Cards, R-Red Cards, G-Green Cards, W-White Cards

3. After they calmed down, they realized that the argument had started because of a simple **misperception**: he thought that she had told him that she would be home in time to eat dinner. What she had really said was, "I think you're a winner."

***How does this word get its meaning from its parts?*: (P30, B7, Y14)**

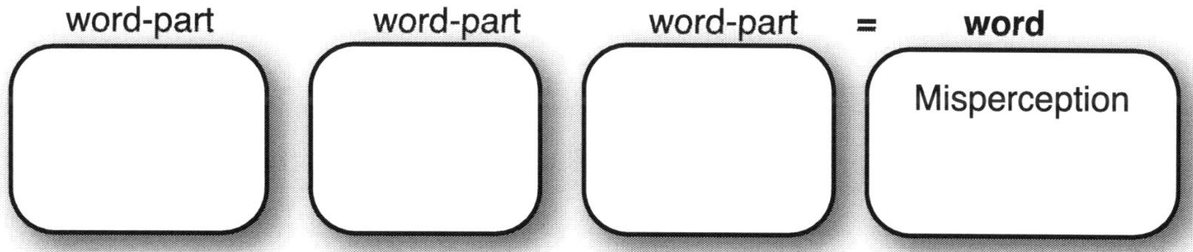

Considering the sentence context and these word-parts, what do you think this word means?
I think that this word means ______________________________
______________________________.

Next, see how close you are to its meaning by consulting the list of definitions.

4. Famous actors try to go out into supermarkets and subways, but they are too **conspicuous** to go unnoticed.

***How does this word get its meaning from its parts?*: (P10, B25, W18)**

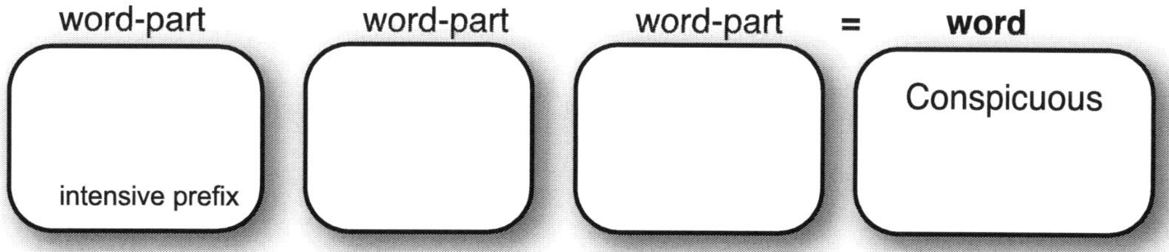

Considering the sentence context and these word-parts, what do you think this word means?
I think that this word means ______________________________
______________________________.

Next, see how close you are to its meaning by consulting the list of definitions.

Hints: P-Purple Cards,Y-Yellow Cards, B-Blue Cards, R-Red Cards, G-Green Cards, W-White Cards

5. It was said that Cleopatra, the ravishing Egyptian Queen, could **seduce** a man and bring him under her power with just one wink of her eye.

***How does this word get its meaning from its parts?*: (B19, Y28)**

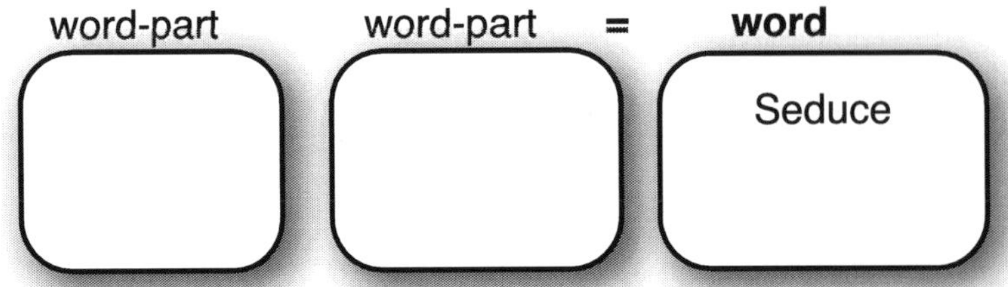

Considering the sentence context and these word-parts, what do you think this word means?
***I think that this word means*____**
____.

Next, see how close you are to its meaning by consulting the list of definitions.

6. The Titanic lies **submerged** at the bottom of the sea.

***How does this word get its meaning from its parts?*: (P45, R16)**

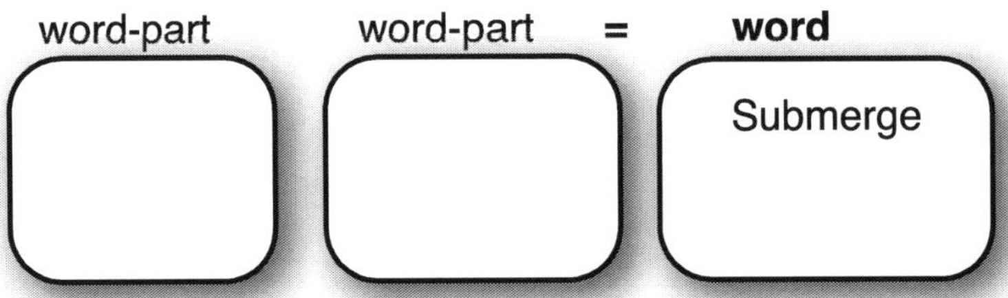

Considering the sentence context and these word-parts, what do you think this word means?
***I think that this word means*____**
____.

Next, see how close you are to its meaning by consulting the list of definitions.

Hints: P-Purple Cards,Y-Yellow Cards, B-Blue Cards, R-Red Cards, G-Green Cards, W-White Cards

7. Older people are more **susceptible** to illnesses unless they keep their bodies in great shape.

***How does this word get its meaning from its parts?* (P45, Y14, W1)**

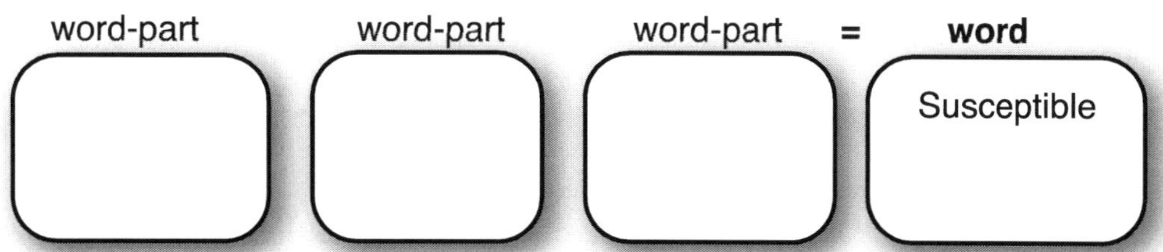

Considering the sentence context and these word-parts, what do you think this word means?
I think that this word means____
____.

Next, see how close you are to its meaning by consulting the list of definitions.

8. Submarines rely on **periscopes** to observe what is happening on the surface.

***How does this word get its meaning from its parts?*: (P39, B17)**

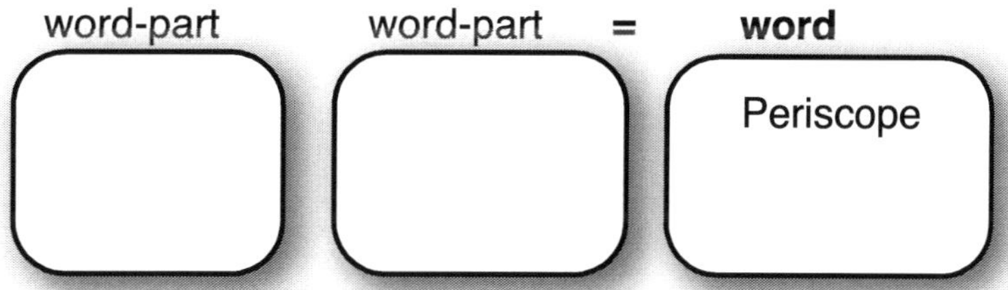

Considering the sentence context and these word-parts, what do you think this word means?
I think that this word means____
____.

Next, see how close you are to its meaning by consulting the list of definitions.

Hints: P-Purple Cards,Y-Yellow Cards, B-Blue Cards, R-Red Cards, G-Green Cards, W-White Cards

9. Every year, the so called "food experts" tell us that something tasty is actually bad for us. Then, only a few months later, these same "experts" produce evidence that **contradict** their original findings. No wonder everyone is confused about what to eat.

***How does this word get its meaning from its parts?*: (Y20, Y27)**

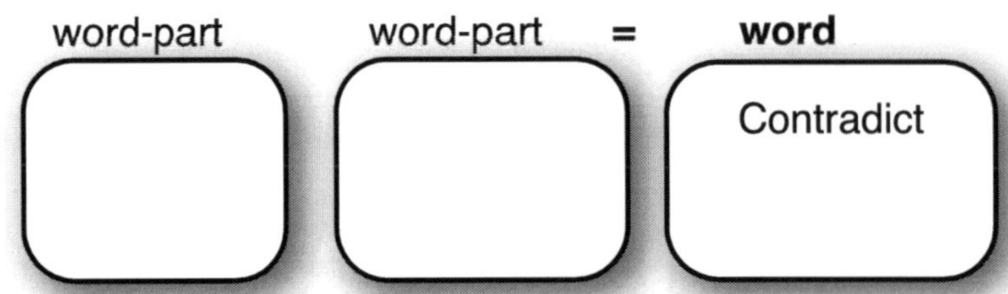

Considering the sentence context and these word-parts, what do you think this word means?
***I think that this word means*______________________________________**
____.

Next, see how close you are to its meaning by consulting the list of definitions.

10. The **biodiversity** of the oceans is astonishing: there are thousands of different life forms, each with varying degrees of spectacular differences.

***How does this word get its meaning from its parts?*: (Y13, P13, G14)**

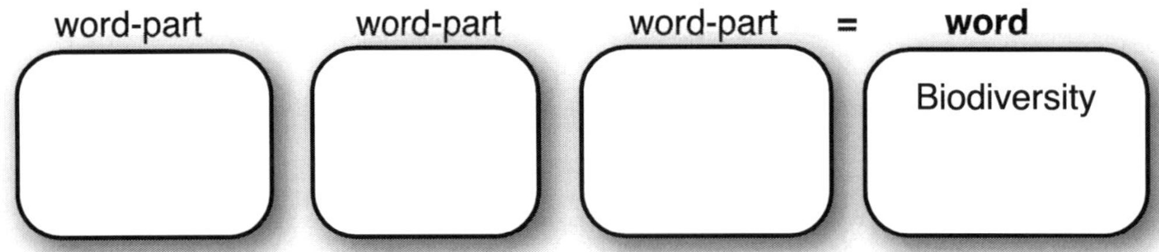

Considering the sentence context and these word-parts, what do you think this word means?
***I think that this word means*______________________________________**
____.

Next, see how close you are to its meaning by consulting the list of definitions.

Hints: P-Purple Cards,Y-Yellow Cards, B-Blue Cards, R-Red Cards, G-Green Cards, W-White Cards

11. School officials **proscribed** the wearing of any clothing with colors that had been adopted by the hostile gangs.

How does this word get its meaning from its parts?: **(P41, B18)**

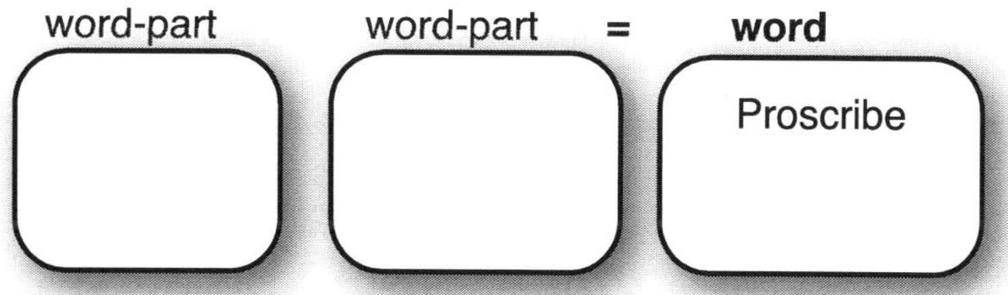

Considering the sentence context and these word-parts, what do you think this word means?
I think that this word means______________________________________
____.

Next, see how close you are to its meaning by consulting the list of definitions.

12. President Woodrow Wilson remained **intransigent** and would not countenance any agreement between him and the Republicans if it meant that he would have to compromise.

How does this word get its meaning from its parts?: **(P25, G7)**

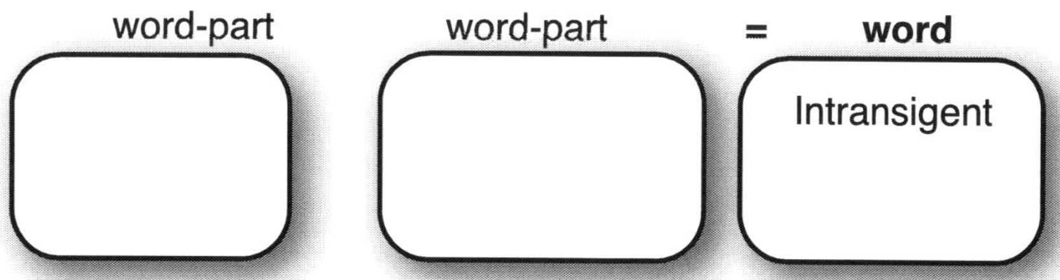

Considering the sentence context and these word-parts, what do you think this word means?
I think that this word means______________________________________
____.

Next, see how close you are to its meaning by consulting the list of definitions.

Hints: P-Purple Cards,Y-Yellow Cards, B-Blue Cards, R-Red Cards, G-Green Cards, W-White Cards

13. The doctor told him that his heart defect was **congenital**, which meant that he had been born with that problem.

***How does this word get its meaning from its parts?*: (P10, R4, W2)**

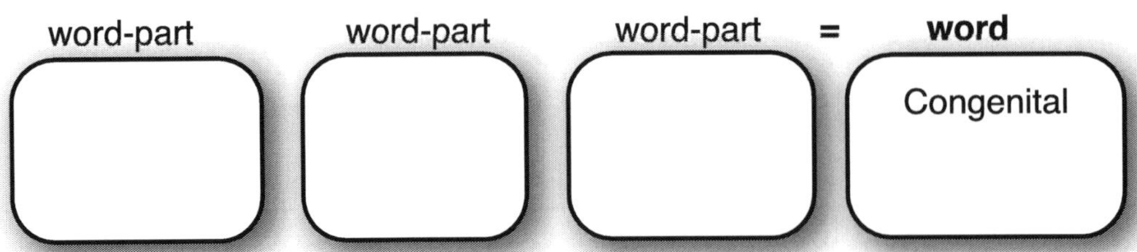

Considering the sentence context and these word-parts, what do you think this word means?
I think that this word means____
____.

Next, see how close you are to its meaning by consulting the list of definitions.

14. Many claimed that the conquering soldiers were **malevolent** and committed cruel acts against the civilian population.

***How does this word get its meaning from its parts?*: (P28, G15)**

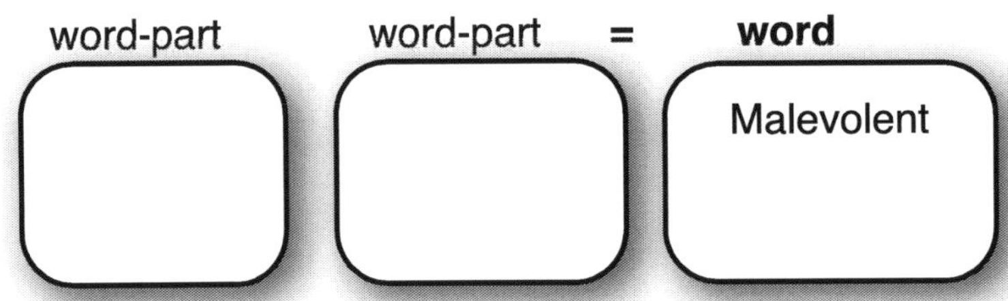

Considering the sentence context and these word-parts, what do you think this word means?
I think that this word means____
____.

Next, see how close you are to its meaning by consulting the list of definitions.

Hints: P-Purple Cards,Y-Yellow Cards, B-Blue Cards, R-Red Cards, G-Green Cards, W-White Cards

15. No matter what the President tried to do, Congress continued to **contravene** all of his policies.

***How does this word get its meaning from its parts?*: (Y20, G12)**

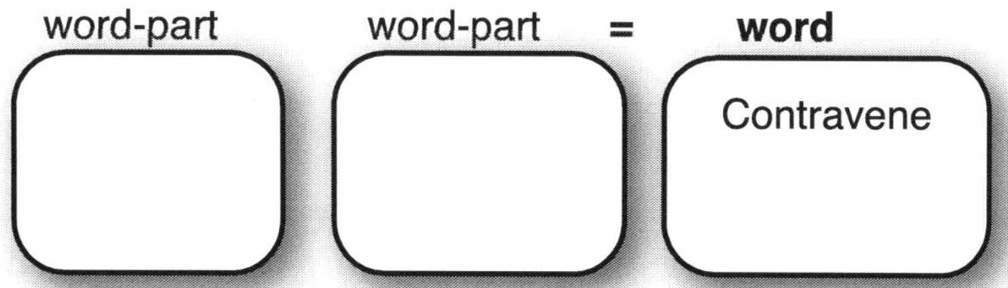

Considering the sentence context and these word-parts, what do you think this word means?
I think that this word means____
____.

Next, see how close you are to its meaning by consulting the list of definitions.

16. The conference **convened** at nine P.M., and all the powerful members were in attendance.

***How does this word get its meaning from its parts?*: (P10, G12)**

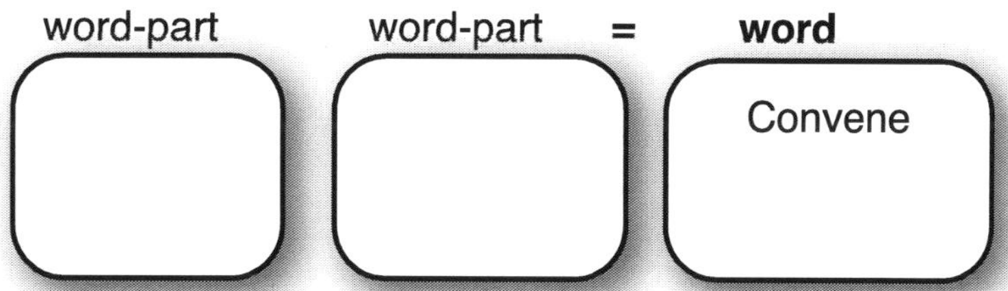

Considering the sentence context and these word-parts, what do you think this word means?
I think that this word means____
____.

Next, see how close you are to its meaning by consulting the list of definitions.

Hints: P-Purple Cards,Y-Yellow Cards, B-Blue Cards, R-Red Cards, G-Green Cards, W-White Cards

17. In **retrospect**, Congress should have denied the President the power to wage a war without a full investigation of its consequences.

***How does this word get its meaning from its parts?*:** **(B15, B25)**

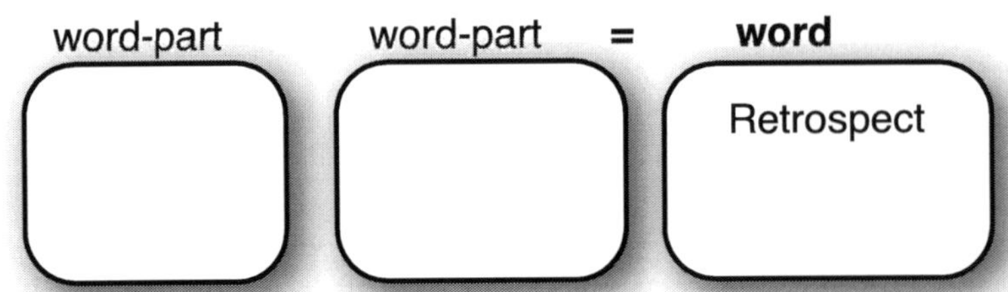

Considering the sentence context and these word-parts, what do you think this word means?
I think that this word means ____

____.

Next, see how close you are to its meaning by consulting the list of definitions.

18. Some religious groups claim that all men need regeneration to live a new life. Christians call it being "born again."

***How does this word get its meaning from its parts?*:** (P43, R4, W11)

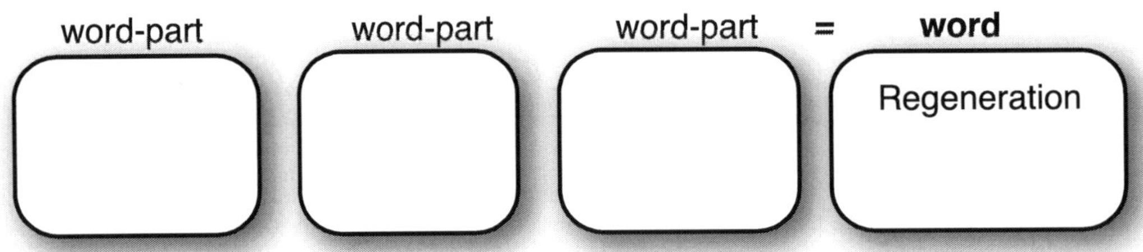

Considering the sentence context and these word-parts, what do you think this word means?
I think that this word means ____

____.

Next, see how close you are to its meaning by consulting the list of definitions.

Hints: P-Purple Cards,Y-Yellow Cards, B-Blue Cards, R-Red Cards, G-Green Cards, W-White Cards

19. After the Civil War, the South passed a series of Jim Crow laws designed to **segregate** blacks from whites.

***How does this word get its meaning from its parts?*: (B19, R6)**

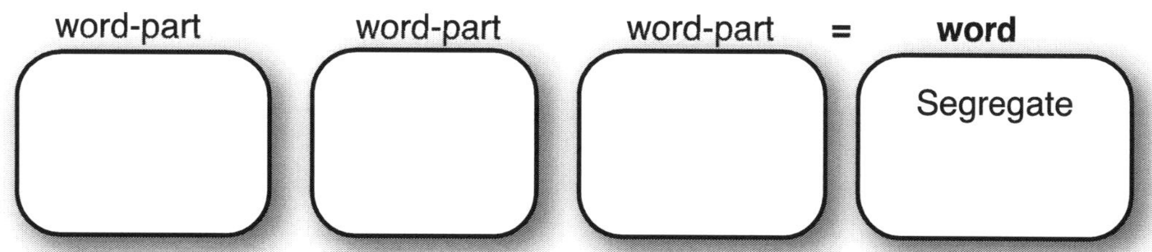

Considering the sentence context and these word-parts, what do you think this word means?
***I think that this word means*____**

____.

Next, see how close you are to its meaning by consulting the list of definitions.

20. After his surgery, the man was urged by doctors to **perambulate** through the gardens outside of the hospital so that he could recover his strength.

***How does this word get its meaning from its parts?*:** (P38, Y3)

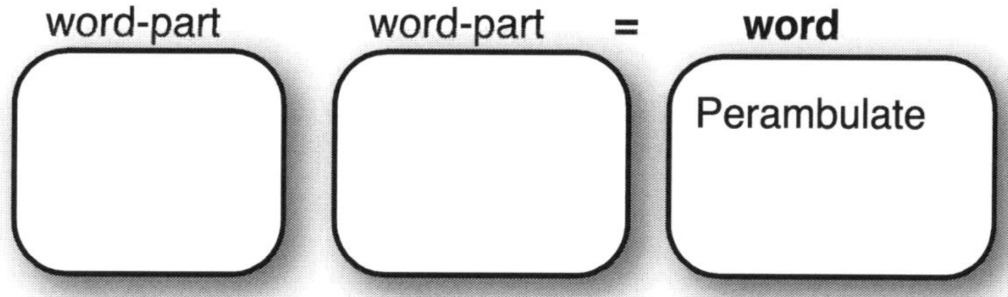

Considering the sentence context and these word-parts, what do you think this word means?
***I think that this word means*____**

____.

Next, see how close you are to its meaning by consulting the list of definitions.

Hints: P-Purple Cards,Y-Yellow Cards, B-Blue Cards, R-Red Cards, G-Green Cards, W-White Cards

21. Mona was not a **bibliophile**: no one could ever accuse her of loving libraries. But during final exam week, she literally lived in the stacks; and, she never stopped reading except for a few trips to the bathroom.

***How does this word get its meaning from its parts?*: (Y12, B8)**

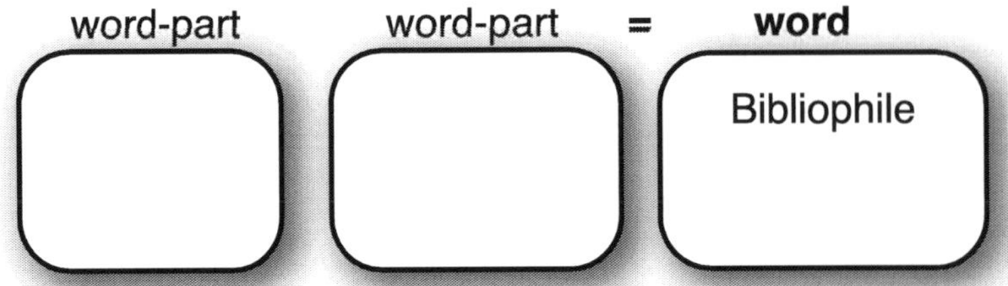

Considering the sentence context and these word-parts, what do you think this word means?
***I think that this word means*___________________________________**
____.

Next, see how close you are to its meaning by consulting the list of definitions.

22. Life is too **transitory** for us to be worried about small things. One day you're here, the next day you're gone.

***How does this word get its meaning from its parts?*: (P48)**

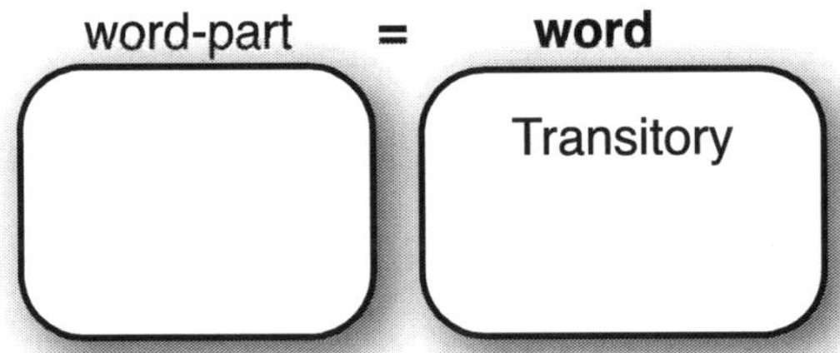

Considering the sentence context and these word-parts, what do you think this word means?
***I think that this word means*___________________________________**
____.

Next, see how close you are to its meaning by consulting the list of definitions.

Hints: P-Purple Cards,Y-Yellow Cards, B-Blue Cards, R-Red Cards, G-Green Cards, W-White Cards

23. England still has a **monarchy**, and the people seem to love their kings and queens.

How does this word get its meaning from its parts?: (P31, W24)

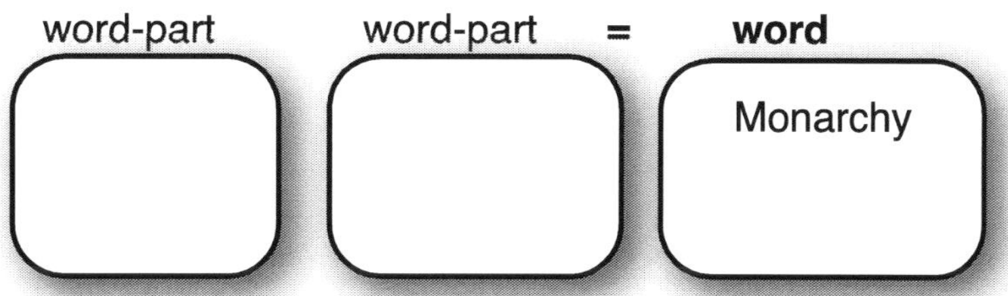

Considering the sentence context and these word-parts, what do you think this word means?
I think that this word means____________________________________
____.

Next, see how close you are to its meaning by consulting the list of definitions.

24. People who love to walk now use their smartphones as **pedometers** so that they can keep an accurate log of how much they have exercised.

How does this word get its meaning from its parts?: **(B6, R17)**

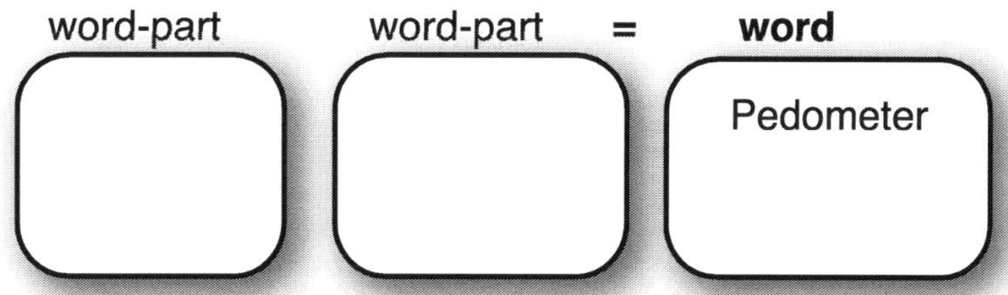

Considering the sentence context and these word-parts, what do you think this word means?
I think that this word means____________________________________
____.

Next, see how close you are to its meaning by consulting the list of definitions.

Hints: P-Purple Cards,Y-Yellow Cards, B-Blue Cards, R-Red Cards, G-Green Cards, W-White Cards

25. Judaism, Christianity, and Islam are the only three **monotheistic** religions. Historically, all other religions have practiced **polytheism**.

***How does the first word get its meaning from its parts?*: (P31, G5)**

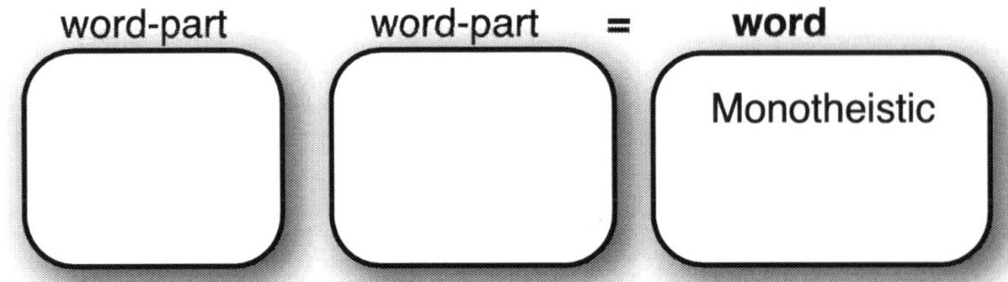

Considering the sentence context and these word-parts, what do you think this word means?
***I think that this word means*______________________________________**
____.

Next, see how close you are to its meaning by consulting the list of definitions.

***How does the second word get its meaning from its parts?*: (P36, G5)**

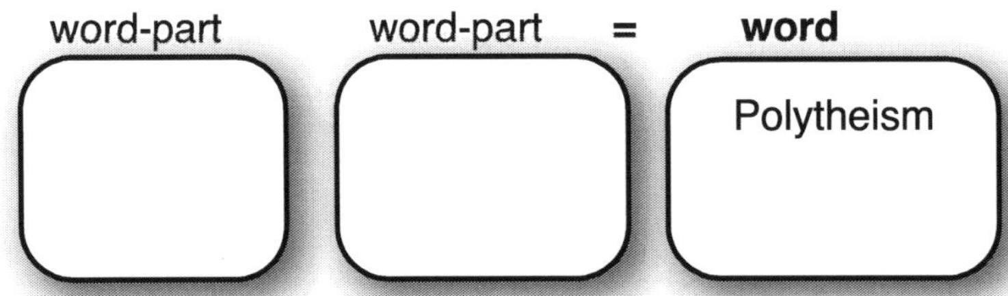

Considering the sentence context and these word-parts, what do you think this word means?
***I think that this word means*______________________________________**
____.

Next, see how close you are to its meaning by consulting the list of definitions.

Hints: P-Purple Cards,Y-Yellow Cards, B-Blue Cards, R-Red Cards, G-Green Cards, W-White Cards

26. Custer's refusal to take the Indians seriously resulted in an **egregious** error of judgement, which left him and his soldiers in an **untenable** situation.

***How does the first word get its meaning from its parts?*: (P15, R6, W18)**

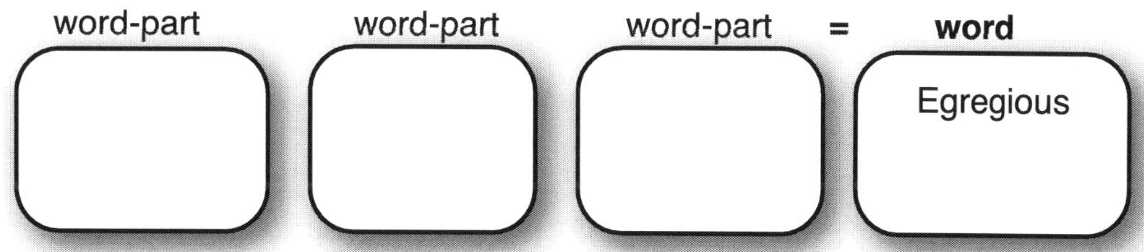

Considering the sentence context and these word-parts, what do you think this word means?
I think that this word means ____
____.

Next, see how close you are to its meaning by consulting the list of definitions.

***How does the second word get its meaning from its parts?*: (P49, G3, W1)**

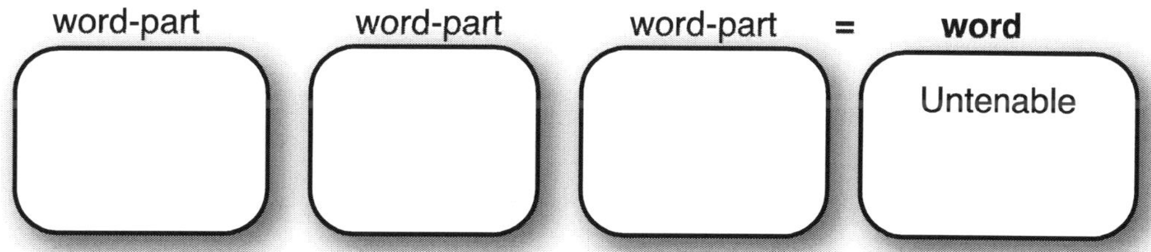

Considering the sentence context and these word-parts, what do you think this word means?
I think that this word means ____
____.

Next, see how close you are to its meaning by consulting the list of definitions.

Hints: P-Purple Cards,Y-Yellow Cards, B-Blue Cards, R-Red Cards, G-Green Cards, W-White Cards

27. Politicians love to practice **circumlocution**: they never get straight to the point.

***How does this word get its meaning from its parts?*: (Y18, R12, W11)**

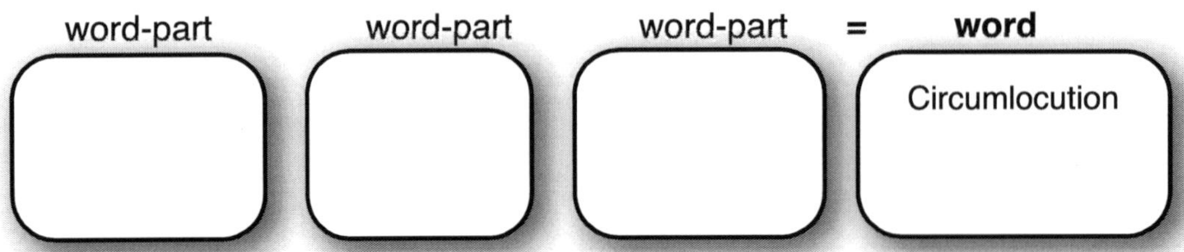

Considering the sentence context and these word-parts, what do you think this word means?
I think that this word means ________________________________
____.

Next, see how close you are to its meaning by consulting the list of definitions.

28. Joan was committed to helping everyone; no wonder she felt so **overextended** and never seemed to have time for herself.

***How does this word get its meaning from its parts?*:** (P35, P15, G2)

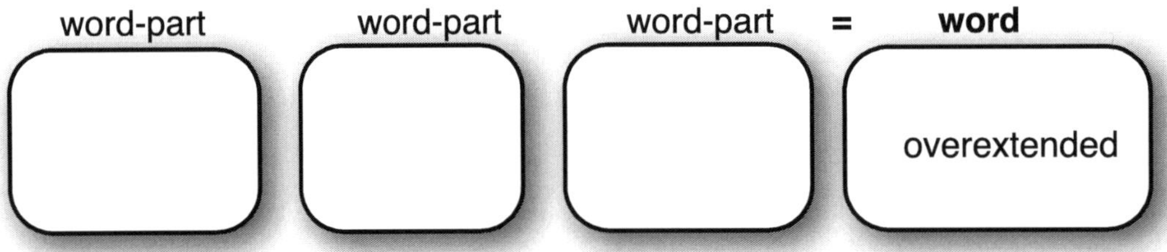

Considering the sentence context and these word-parts, what do you think this word means?
I think that this word means ________________________________
____.

Next, see how close you are to its meaning by consulting the list of definitions.

Hints: P-Purple Cards,Y-Yellow Cards, B-Blue Cards, R-Red Cards, G-Green Cards, W-White Cards

29. He never attended any social gatherings and stayed far from people. He was **misanthropic**, and he wanted everyone to feel his bitter **antipathy** towards them.

How does the first word get its meaning from its parts?: (P30, Y7)

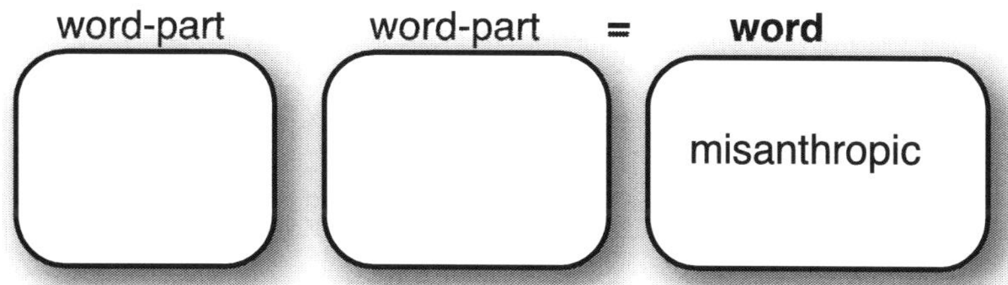

Considering the sentence context and these word-parts, what do you think this word means?
I think that this word means____________________________________
____.

Next, see how close you are to its meaning by consulting the list of definitions.

How does the second word get its meaning from its parts?: (P6, W26)

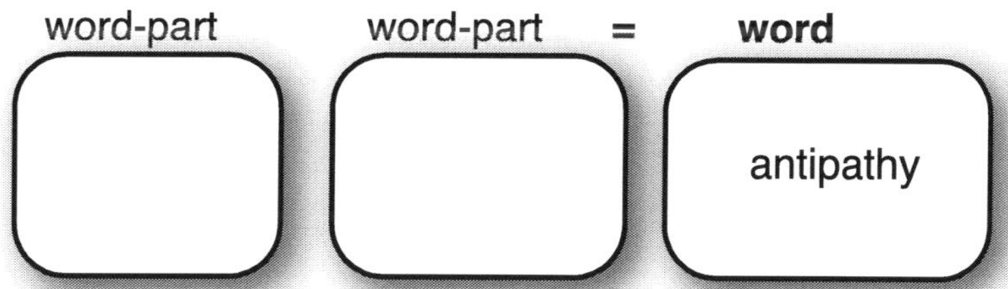

Considering the sentence context and these word-parts, what do you think this word means?
I think that this word means____________________________________
____.

Next, see how close you are to its meaning by consulting the list of definitions.

Hints: P-Purple Cards,Y-Yellow Cards, B-Blue Cards, R-Red Cards, G-Green Cards, W-White Cards

30. When his teacher called him the most **loquacious** child she had ever met, Bob thought that she was trying to compliment him; he didn't know that she was trying to get him to keep his mouth shut for a few seconds.

***How does this word get its meaning from its parts?*: (R12, W18)**

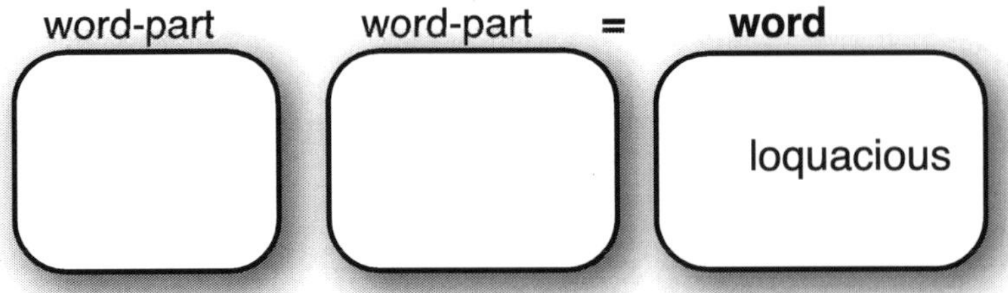

Considering the sentence context and these word-parts, what do you think this word means?
I think that this word means ____
____.

Next, see how close you are to its meaning by consulting the list of definitions.

Hints: P-Purple Cards,Y-Yellow Cards, B-Blue Cards, R-Red Cards, G-Green Cards, W-White Cards

31. While his sister was shy and reticent, he was **extroverted** and **gregarious**: everyone knew that he was the life of the party.

***How does the first word get its meaning from its parts?*: (P21, G14)**

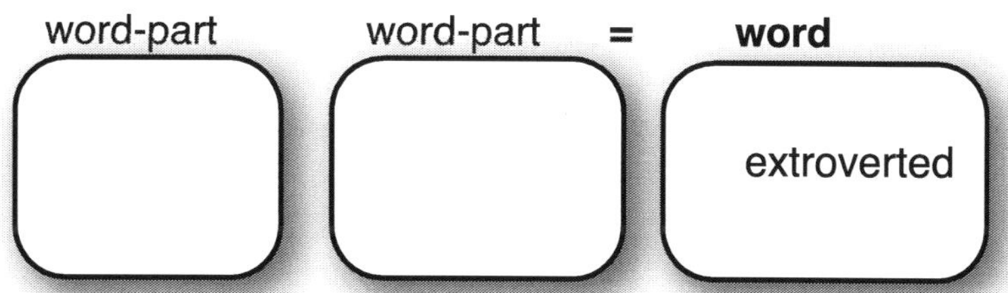

Considering the sentence context and these word-parts, what do you think this word means?
I think that this word means ____
____.

Next, see how close you are to its meaning by consulting the list of definitions.

***How does the second word get its meaning from its parts?:* (R6, W18)**

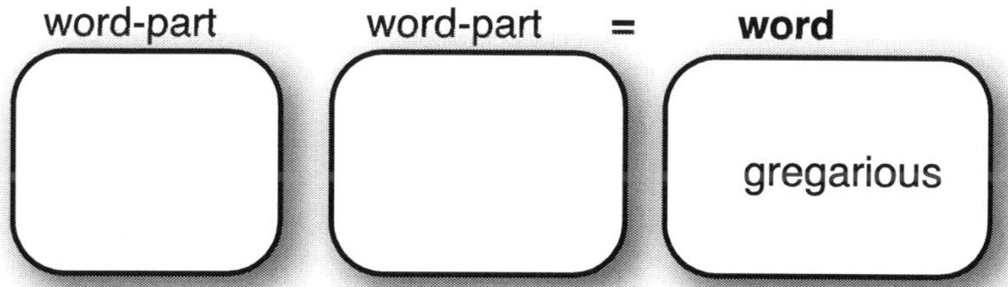

Considering the sentence context and these word-parts, what do you think this word means?
I think that this word means ____
____.

Next, see how close you are to its meaning by consulting the list of definitions.

Hints: P-Purple Cards,Y-Yellow Cards, B-Blue Cards, R-Red Cards, G-Green Cards, W-White Cards

32. Parents urge their children to be **circumspect** when they travel in lonely places, especially after dark.

***How does this word get its meaning from its parts?*: (Y18, B25)**

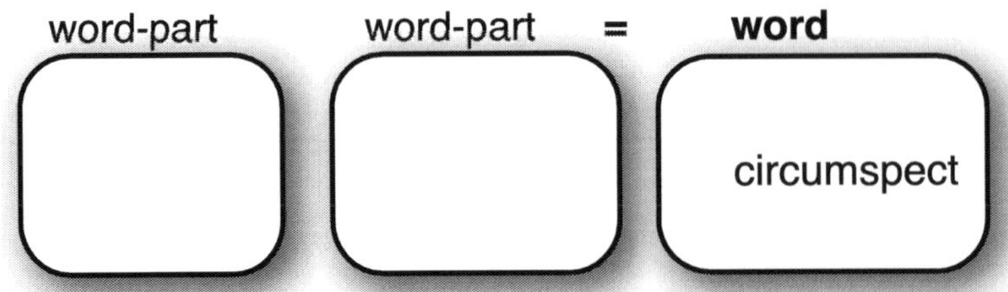

Considering the sentence context and these word-parts, what do you think this word means?
I think that this word means ____
____.

Next, see how close you are to its meaning by consulting the list of definitions.

33. The principal issued an **edict** that prohibited teens from wearing baggy pants below their waists.

***How does this word get its meaning from its parts?*: (P15, Y27)**

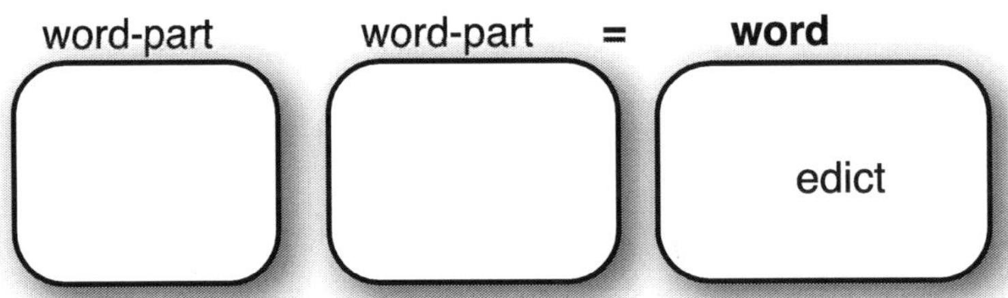

Considering the sentence context and these word-parts, what do you think this word means?
I think that this word means ____
____.

Next, see how close you are to its meaning by consulting the list of definitions.

Hints: P-Purple Cards,Y-Yellow Cards, B-Blue Cards, R-Red Cards, G-Green Cards, W-White Cards

34. She used words like **projectiles**--hurling them violently against her critics, or those who would dare oppose any of her theories.

***How does this word get its meaning from its parts?*: (P41, R9)**

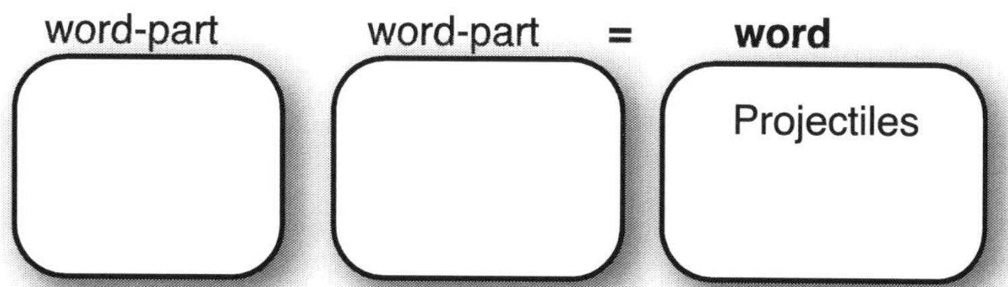

Considering the sentence context and these word-parts, what do you think this word means?
***I think that this word means*______________________________________**

____.

Next, see how close you are to its meaning by consulting the list of definitions.

35. The villagers felt that some **omnipotent** being controlled their destinies. They were completely subservient to its will.

***How does this word get its meaning from its parts?*: (B2, W31)**

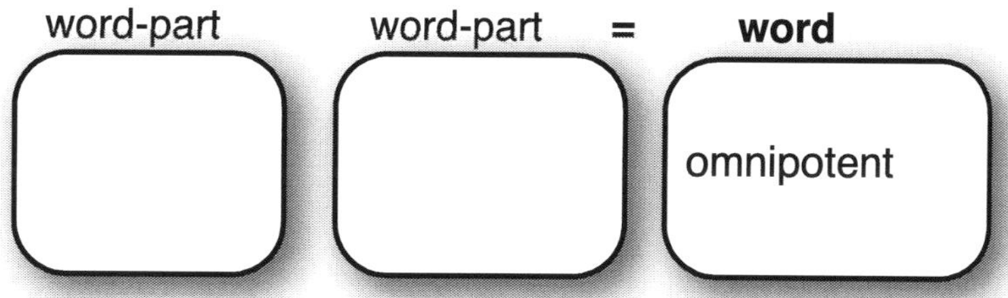

Considering the sentence context and these word-parts, what do you think this word means?
***I think that this word means*______________________________________**

____.

Next, see how close you are to its meaning by consulting the list of definitions.

Hints: P-Purple Cards,Y-Yellow Cards, B-Blue Cards, R-Red Cards, G-Green Cards, W-White Cards

36. Because humans lack **omniscience**, we can never be absolutely certain about everything.

***How does this word get its meaning from its parts?*: (B2, B16)**

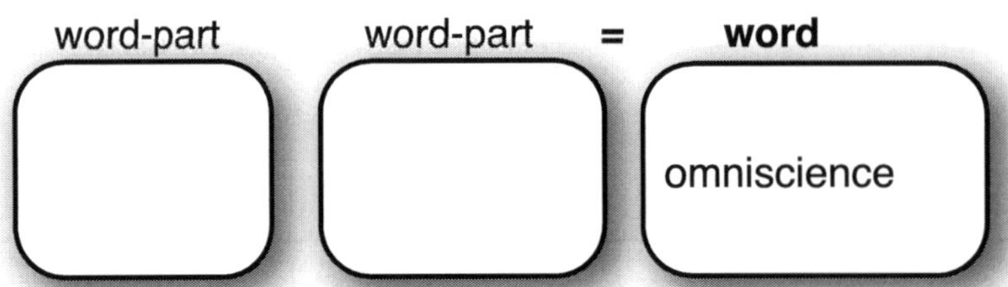

Considering the sentence context and these word-parts, what do you think this word means?
***I think that this word means*____**
____.

Next, see how close you are to its meaning by consulting the list of definitions.

37. What an **obdurate** boy he was. Even his mother called him hard-headed.

***How does this word get its meaning from its parts?*: (P34, W28)**

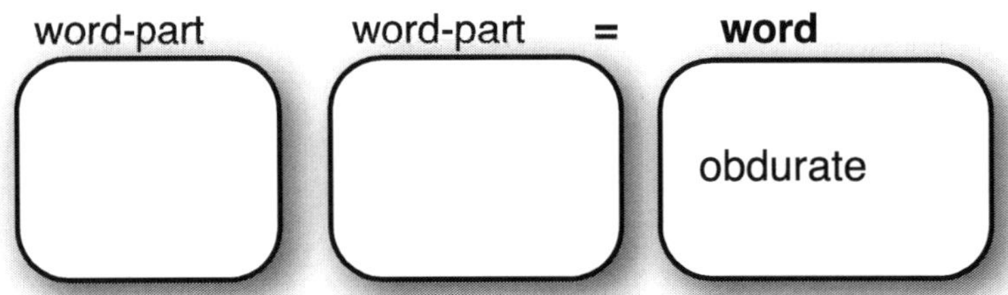

Considering the sentence context and these word-parts, what do you think this word means?
***I think that this word means*____**
____.

Next, see how close you are to its meaning by consulting the list of definitions.

Hints: P-Purple Cards,Y-Yellow Cards, B-Blue Cards, R-Red Cards, G-Green Cards, W-White Cards

38. After hundreds of hours of writing, the **manuscript** was finally complete.

***How does this word get its meaning from its parts?*: (R14, B18)**

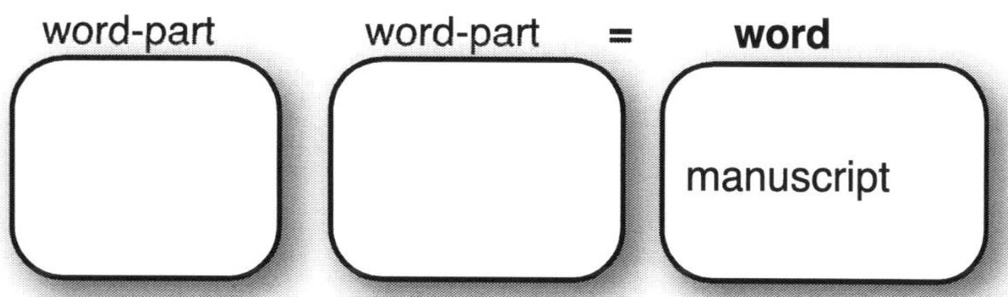

Considering the sentence context and these word-parts, what do you think this word means?
I think that this word means ____
____.

Next, see how close you are to its meaning by consulting the list of definitions.

39. All the evidence seemed to **implicate** Jerald in the robbery, but he claimed that the evidence was only circumstantial.

***How does this word get its meaning from its parts?*: (P16, B11)**

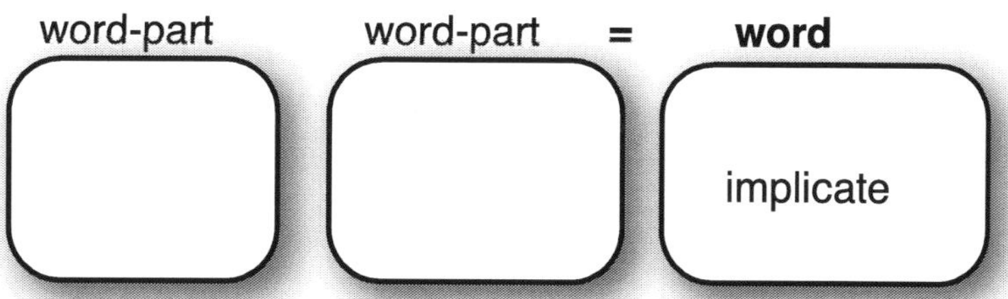

Considering the sentence context and these word-parts, what do you think this word means?
I think that this word means ____
____.

Next, see how close you are to its meaning by consulting the list of definitions.

Hints: P-Purple Cards,Y-Yellow Cards, B-Blue Cards, R-Red Cards, G-Green Cards, W-White Cards

40. The child told his mother that he was unable to do his homework because his teacher had simply assigned an **insuperable** amount of work to do in one night.

***How does this word get its meaning from its parts?*: (P25, P46, W1)**

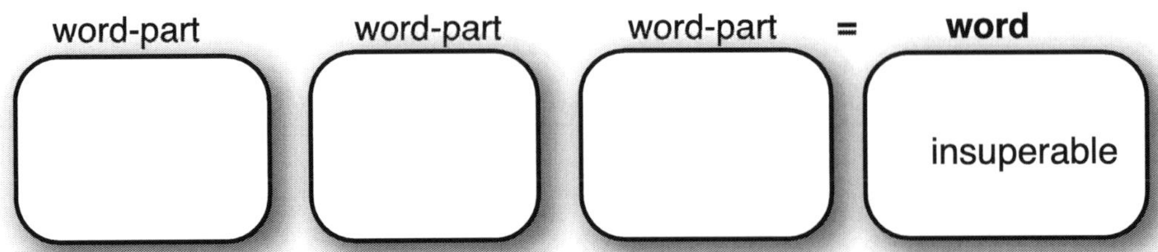

Considering the sentence context and these word-parts, what do you think this word means?
I think that this word means ____
____.

Next, see how close you are to its meaning by consulting the list of definitions.

41. Cynthia's **retention** of facts was amazing: she never seemed to forget anything.

***How does this word get its meaning from its parts?*: (P43, G2, W11)**

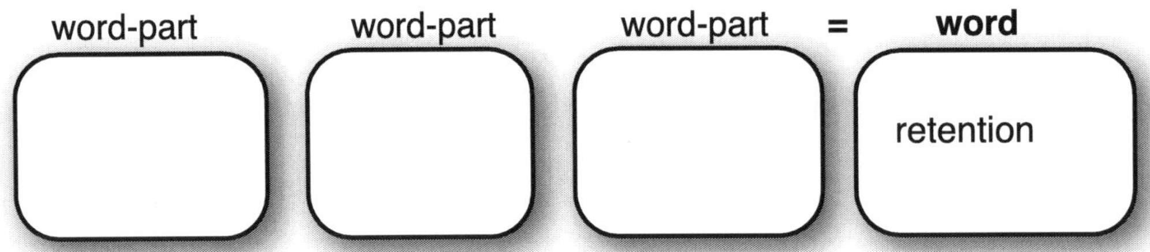

Considering the sentence context and these word-parts, what do you think this word means?
I think that this word means ____
____.

Next, see how close you are to its meaning by consulting the list of definitions.

Hints: P-Purple Cards,Y-Yellow Cards, B-Blue Cards, R-Red Cards, G-Green Cards, W-White Cards

42. It's certainly good to be **introspective** at times: it's important to look deeply into one's own heart to understand one's own motives and emotions.

***How does this word get its meaning from its parts?*: (R8, B25)**

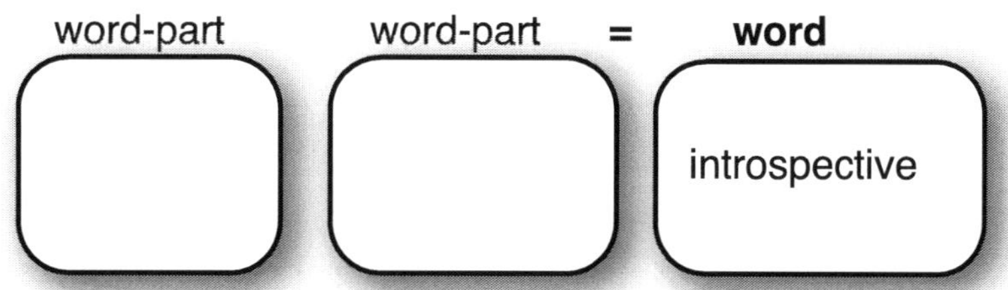

Considering the sentence context and these word-parts, what do you think this word means?
***I think that this word means*____**
____.

Next, see how close you are to its meaning by consulting the list of definitions.

43. The spies **intercepted** the message that was sent from the terrorist to his followers, and they used it to bring him to justice.

***How does this word get its meaning from its parts?*: (P26, Y14)**

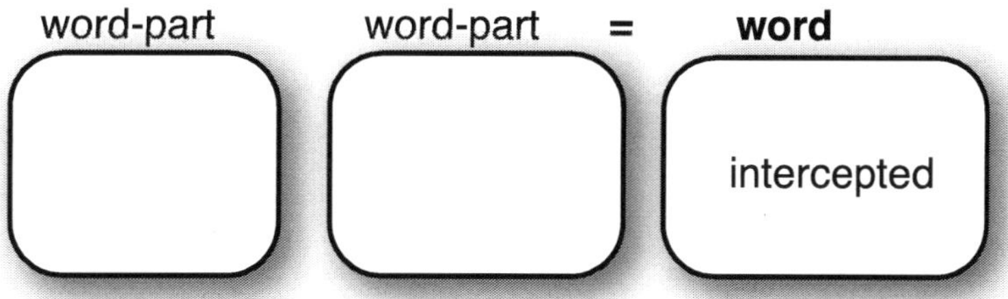

Considering the sentence context and these word-parts, what do you think this word means?
***I think that this word means*____**
____.

Next, see how close you are to its meaning by consulting the list of definitions.

Hints: P-Purple Cards,Y-Yellow Cards, B-Blue Cards, R-Red Cards, G-Green Cards, W-White Cards

44. His doctor ordered him to **abstain** from fatty meats and sugars.

***How does this word get its meaning from its parts?*: (P2, G3)**

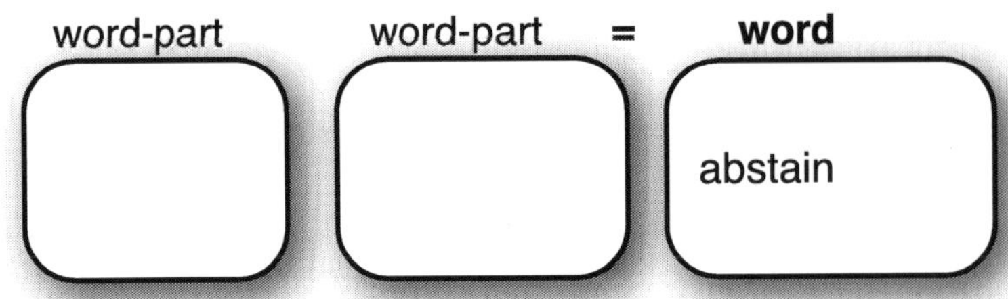

Considering the sentence context and these word-parts, what do you think this word means?
I think that this word means ____________________________________
____.

Next, see how close you are to its meaning by consulting the list of definitions.

45. The **interminable** tribal conflict had lasted for over 200 years and showed no signs of ending.

***How does this word get its meaning from its parts?*: (P25, W33, W1)**

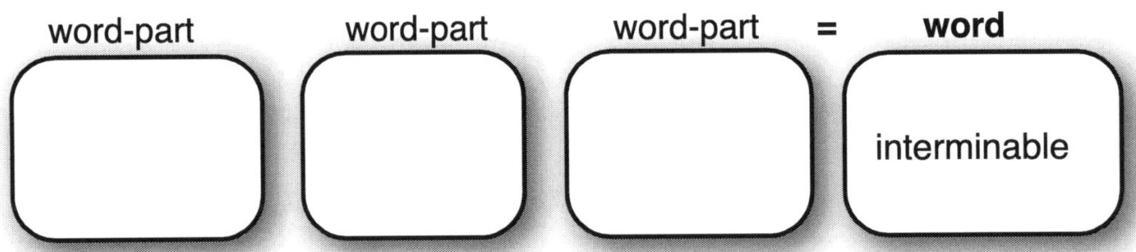

Considering the sentence context and these word-parts, what do you think this word means?
I think that this word means ____________________________________
____.

Next, see how close you are to its meaning by consulting the list of definitions.

Hints: P-Purple Cards,Y-Yellow Cards, B-Blue Cards, R-Red Cards, G-Green Cards, W-White Cards

46. As Jim grew older, his hairline began to **<u>recede</u>**. He knew that he would be completely bald in just a few years.

***How does this word get its meaning from its parts?*: (P43, Y16)**

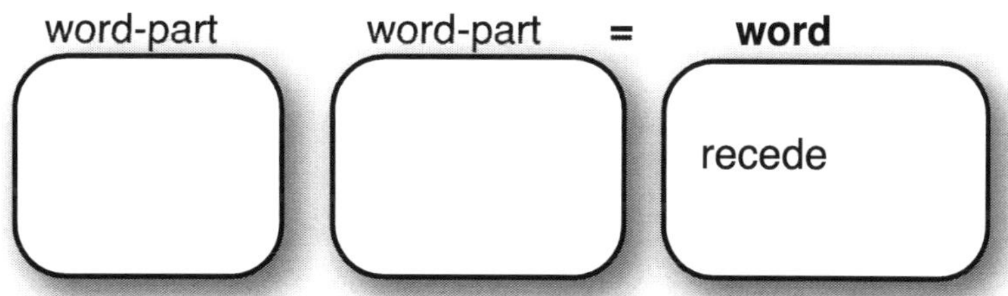

Considering the sentence context and these word-parts, what do you think this word means?
***I think that this word means*____________________________________**
____.

Next, see how close you are to its meaning by consulting the list of definitions.

47. She was our favorite professor because she was able to **<u>explicate</u>** the most complex subjects and help us to easily understand them.

***How does this word get its meaning from its parts?*: (P15, B11)**

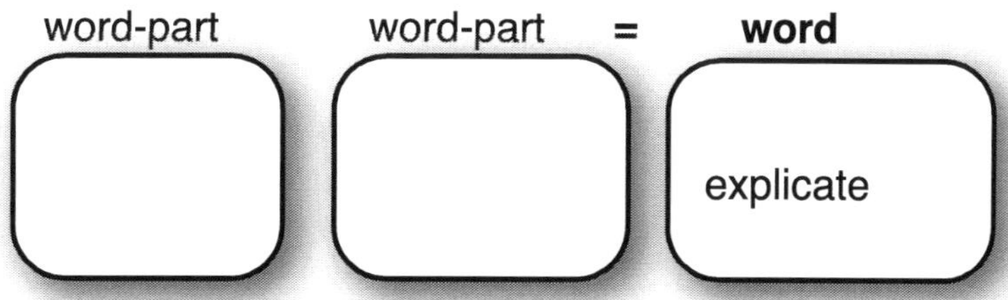

Considering the sentence context and these word-parts, what do you think this word means?
***I think that this word means*____________________________________**
____.

Next, see how close you are to its meaning by consulting the list of definitions.

Hints: P-Purple Cards,Y-Yellow Cards, B-Blue Cards, R-Red Cards, G-Green Cards, W-White Cards

48. No matter how hard they tried, the political parties could not reach an **accord**; instead, the meeting ended in a **discordant** manner.

***How does the first word get its meaning from its parts?*: (P3, Y21)**

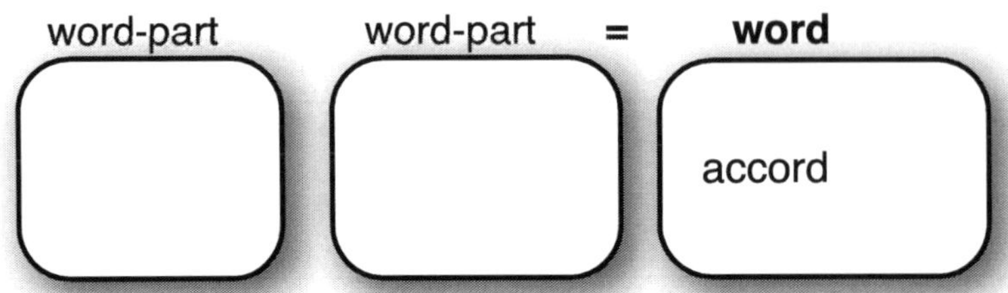

Considering the sentence context and these word-parts, what do you think this word means?
***I think that this word means*_______________________________________**

____.

Next, see how close you are to its meaning by consulting the list of definitions.

***How does the second word get its meaning from its parts?*: (P13, Y21)**

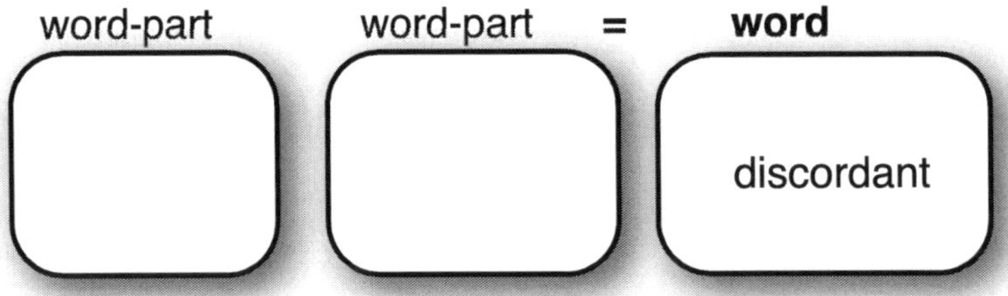

Considering the sentence context and these word-parts, what do you think this word means?
***I think that this word means*_______________________________________**

____.

Next, see how close you are to its meaning by consulting the list of definitions.

Hints: P-Purple Cards,Y-Yellow Cards, B-Blue Cards, R-Red Cards, G-Green Cards, W-White Cards

49. It would take years for any sense of **concord** to exist between the bellicose and discordant leaders again.

***How does this word get its meaning from its parts?*: (P10, Y21)**

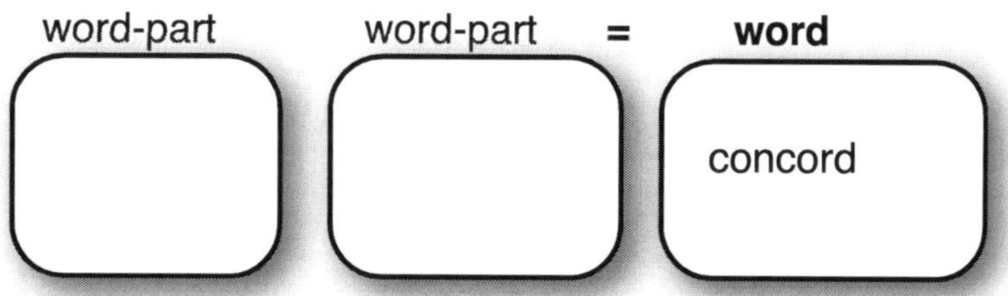

Considering the sentence context and these word-parts, what do you think this word means?
I think that this word means ________________________________
____.

Next, see how close you are to its meaning by consulting the list of definitions.

50. His professor reminded him that the words "same" and "exact" should never be used together since they represented a classic example of a **redundancy**.

***How does this word get its meaning from its parts?* (P43, G8, W20)**

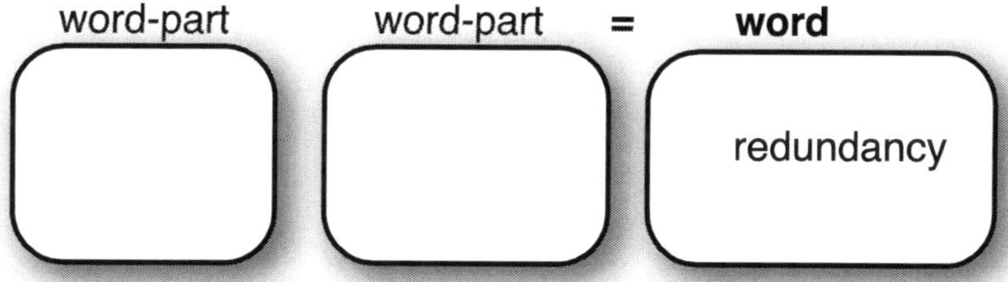

Considering the sentence context and these word-parts, what do you think this word means?
I think that this word means ________________________________
____.

Next, see how close you are to its meaning by consulting the list of definitions.

Hints: P-Purple Cards,Y-Yellow Cards, B-Blue Cards, R-Red Cards, G-Green Cards, W-White Cards

51. It was **<u>inconceivable</u>** to many that America could lose a war to a small country like Vietnam.

***How does this word get its meaning from its parts?*: (P25, P10, Y14)**

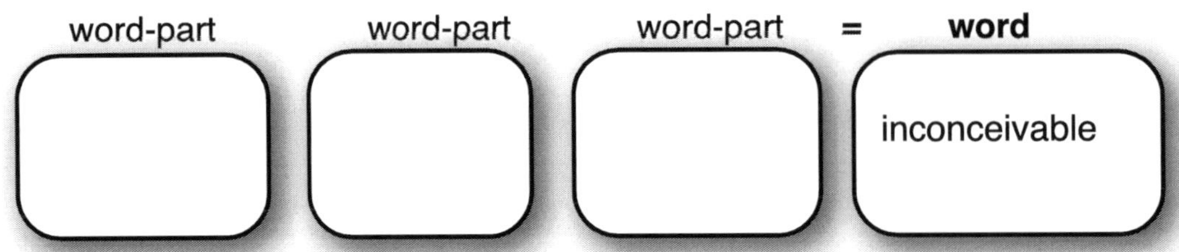

Considering the sentence context and these word-parts, what do you think this word means?
I think that this word means ______________________________________
____.

Next, see how close you are to its meaning by consulting the list of definitions.

52. No one was **<u>prescient</u>** enough to see that Hurricane Sandy would occur; no one thought that such a catastrophe could ever happen in the United States.

***How does this word get its meaning from its parts?*: (P40, B16)**

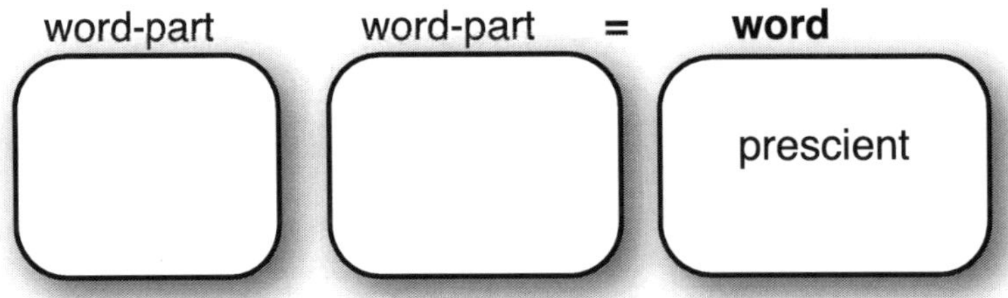

Considering the sentence context and these word-parts, what do you think this word means?
I think that this word means ______________________________________
____.

Next, see how close you are to its meaning by consulting the list of definitions.

Hints: P-Purple Cards,Y-Yellow Cards, B-Blue Cards, R-Red Cards, G-Green Cards, W-White Cards

53. Though some had stubbornly believed that the sun revolved around the earth, science has provided **incontrovertible** evidence that it is the earth that revolves around the sun.

***How does this word get its meaning from its parts?*: (P25, Y20, G14)**

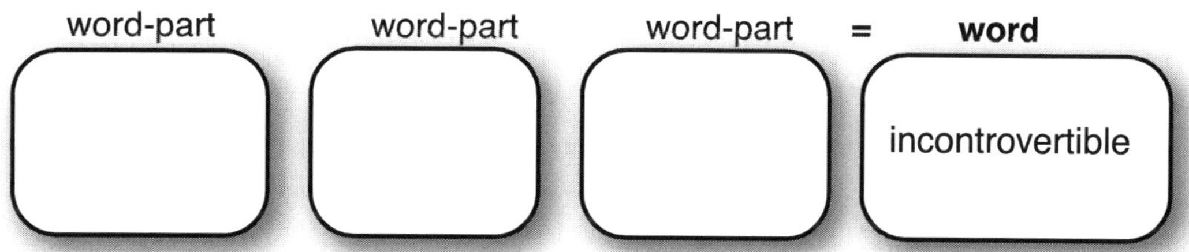

Considering the sentence context and these word-parts, what do you think this word means?
I think that this word means____
____.

Next, see how close you are to its meaning by consulting the list of definitions.

54. Larry made his feelings clear: he was **unambiguous** in his support for the President. There was never any shred of doubt or wavering in any of his public statements concerning the President's reelection.

***How does this word get its meaning from its parts?*: (P49, Y2)**

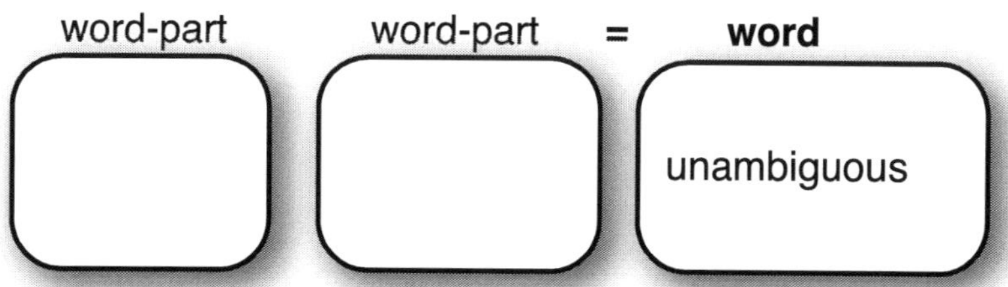

Considering the sentence context and these word-parts, what do you think this word means?
I think that this word means____
____.

Next, see how close you are to its meaning by consulting the list of definitions.

Hints: P-Purple Cards,Y-Yellow Cards, B-Blue Cards, R-Red Cards, G-Green Cards, W-White Cards

55. Even though he had been knocked down several times, the **tenacious** fighter kept getting off the canvas to fight one more round.

***How does this word get its meaning from its parts?*: (G3, B3)**

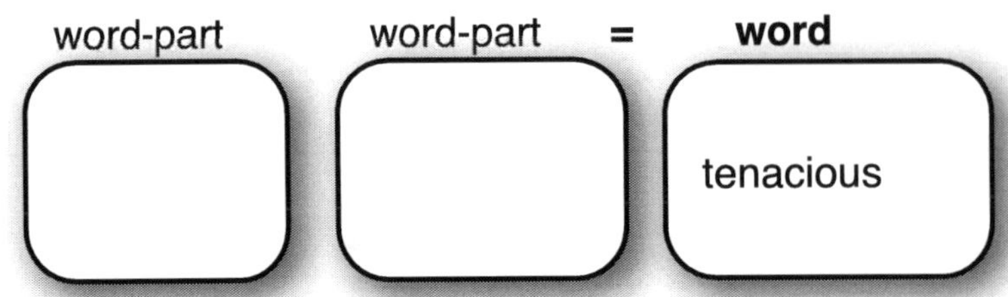

Considering the sentence context and these word-parts, what do you think this word means?
***I think that this word means*____**
____.

Next, see how close you are to its meaning by consulting the list of definitions.

56. Because Jerome had such a **perspicacious** mind, he was able to **perceive** that his so-called friends were really intending to mislead him.

***How does the first word get its meaning from its parts?*: (P38, B25, W28)**

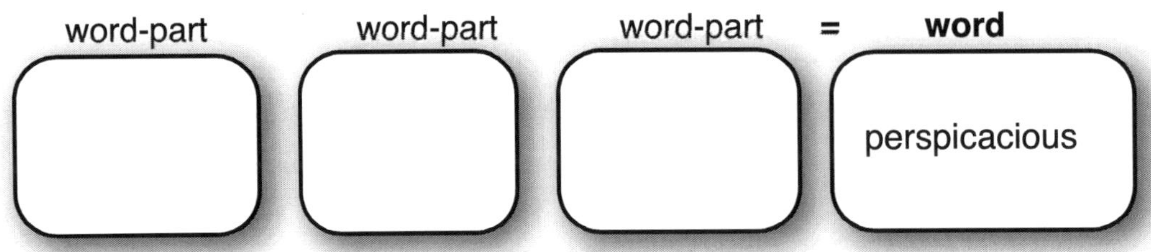

Considering the sentence context and these word-parts, what do you think this word means?
***I think that this word means*____**
____.

Next, see how close you are to its meaning by consulting the list of definitions.

Hints: P-Purple Cards,Y-Yellow Cards, B-Blue Cards, R-Red Cards, G-Green Cards, W-White Cards

***How does the second word get its meaning from its parts?*: (P38, Y14)**

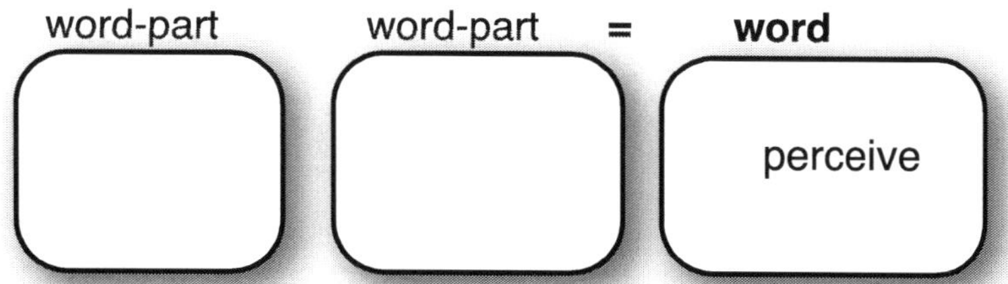

Considering the sentence context and these word-parts, what do you think this word means?
I think that this word means____
____.

Next, see how close you are to its meaning by consulting the list of definitions.

57. We should all **aspire** to be the best that we can be.

How does this word get its meaning from its parts?: (P3, B26)

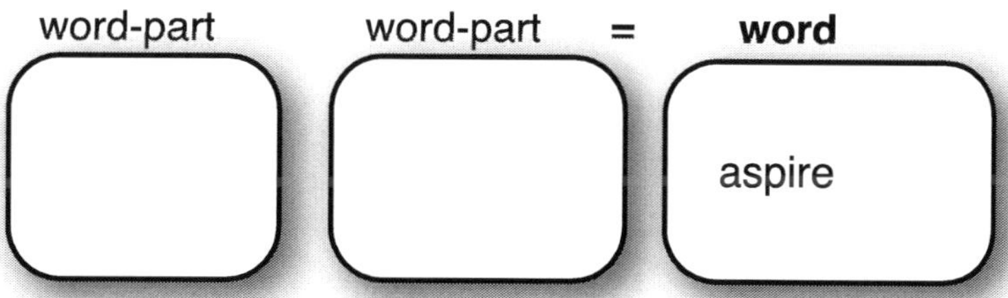

Considering the sentence context and these word-parts, what do you think this word means?
I think that this word means____
____.

Next, see how close you are to its meaning by consulting the list of definitions.

Hints: P-Purple Cards,Y-Yellow Cards, B-Blue Cards, R-Red Cards, G-Green Cards, W-White Cards

58. After the Civil War, those who had lived in the **antebellum** South longed for what they mistakenly called the "good old days."

***How does this word get its meaning from its parts?*: (Y6, Y10)**

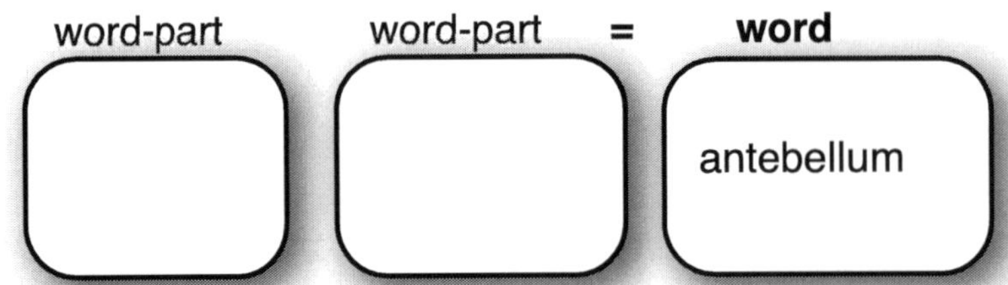

Considering the sentence context and these word-parts, what do you think this word means?
I think that this word means ____
____.

Next, see how close you are to its meaning by consulting the list of definitions.

59. The dictator claimed that he had created a(n) **autocracy**, where he ruled with total power because he feared that the country would fall into a state of **anarchy** and confusion.

***How does the first word get its meaning from its parts?*: (Y9, W24)**

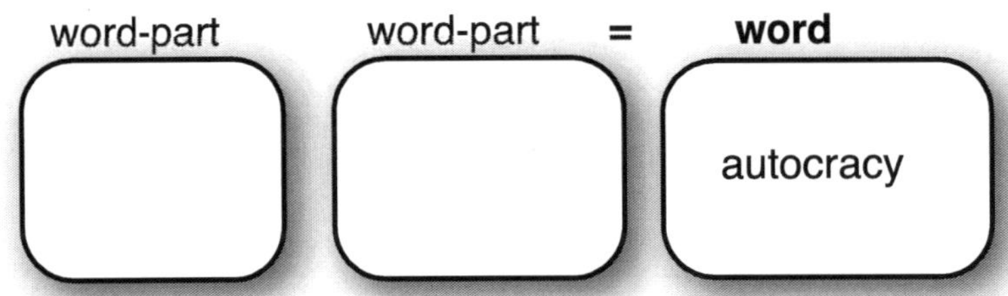

Considering the sentence context and these word-parts, what do you think this word means?
I think that this word means ____
____.

Next, see how close you are to its meaning by consulting the list of definitions.

Hints: P-Purple Cards,Y-Yellow Cards, B-Blue Cards, R-Red Cards, G-Green Cards, W-White Cards

***How does the second word get its meaning from its parts?*: (P1, W24)**

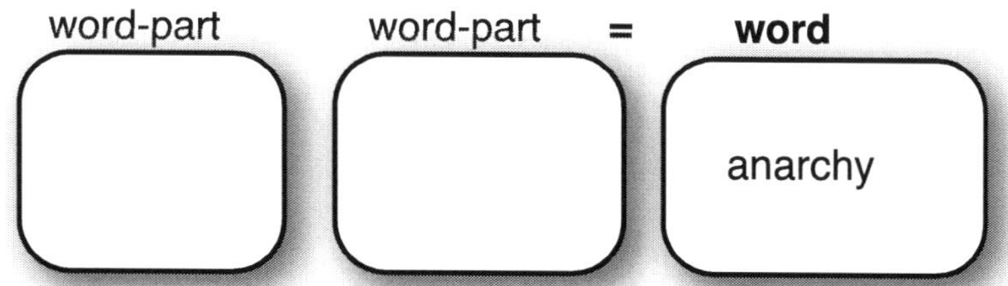

Considering the sentence context and these word-parts, what do you think this word means?
***I think that this word means*______________________________**
____.

Next, see how close you are to its meaning by consulting the list of definitions.

60. Though his soldiers had told him to avoid the fierce enemy, Alexander rushed headlong into a thoughtless and dangerous decision and placed his entire army on the **precipice** of destruction.

***How does this word get its meaning from its parts?:* (P40, Y15)**

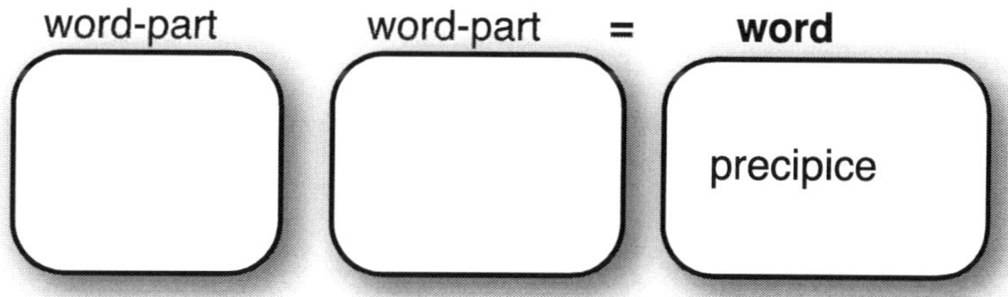

Considering the sentence context and these word-parts, what do you think this word means?
***I think that this word means*______________________________**
____.

Next, see how close you are to its meaning by consulting the list of definitions.

Hints: P-Purple Cards,Y-Yellow Cards, B-Blue Cards, R-Red Cards, G-Green Cards, W-White Cards

61. The rival political campaign used dirty tactics and **disinformation**, which made it seem as if the governor were a criminal.

***How does this word get its meaning from its parts?*: (P13, P16, R2)**

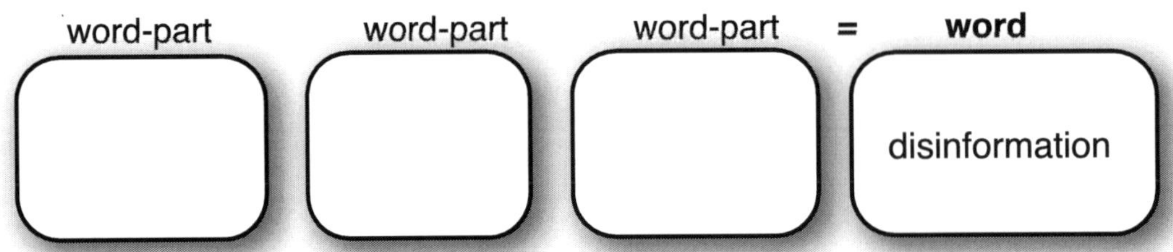

Considering the sentence context and these word-parts, what do you think this word means?
I think that this word means ____
____.

Next, see how close you are to its meaning by consulting the list of definitions.

62. She was detained at the airport for two hours and became **dejected** because she felt that she would never reach her destination.

***How does this word get its meaning from its parts?*: (P11, R9)**

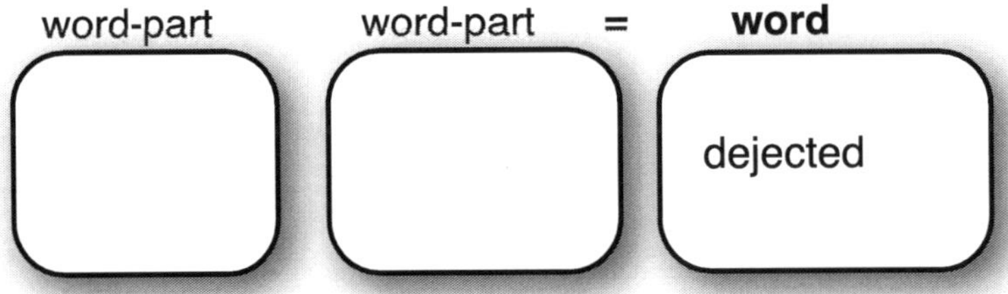

Considering the sentence context and these word-parts, what do you think this word means?
I think that this word means ____
____.

Next, see how close you are to its meaning by consulting the list of definitions.

Hints: P-Purple Cards,Y-Yellow Cards, B-Blue Cards, R-Red Cards, G-Green Cards, W-White Cards

63. There is a difference between being obedient and being **subservient**. Obedience means knowing your duty, while the latter means acting like a servant.

How does this word get its meaning from its parts?: (P45, W32)

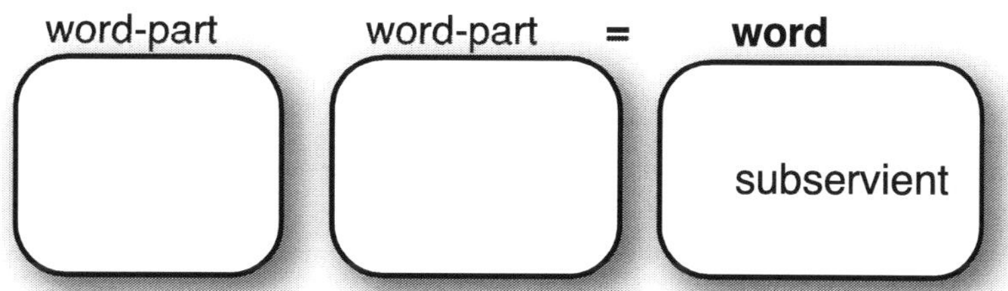

Considering the sentence context and these word-parts, what do you think this word means?
I think that this word means____________________________________
____.

Next, see how close you are to its meaning by consulting the list of definitions.

64. Every good teacher wants to **disseminate** truth to as many young people as possible.

How does this word get its meaning from its parts?: **(P13, B20)**

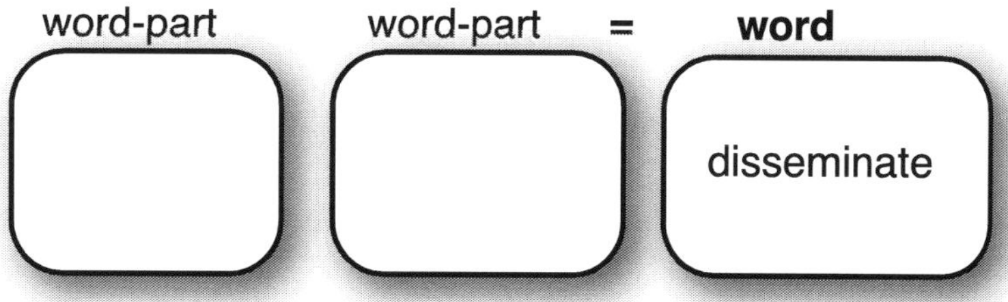

Considering the sentence context and these word-parts, what do you think this word means?
I think that this word means____________________________________
____.

Next, see how close you are to its meaning by consulting the list of definitions.

Hints: P-Purple Cards,Y-Yellow Cards, B-Blue Cards, R-Red Cards, G-Green Cards, W-White Cards

65. After a large meal, your stomach can easily become **distended**.

***How does this word get its meaning from its parts?*: (P13, G2)**

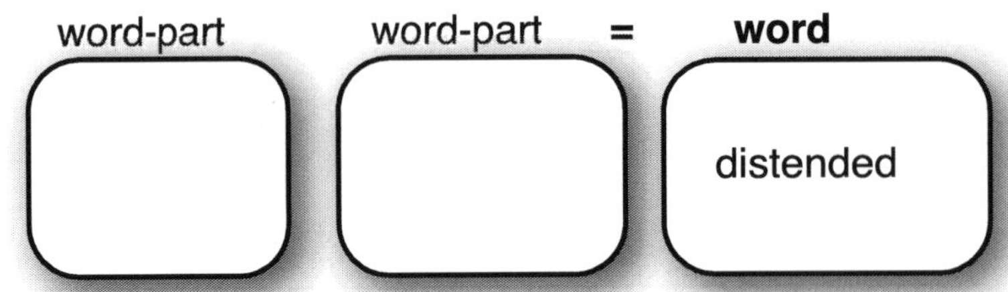

Considering the sentence context and these word-parts, what do you think this word means?
***I think that this word means*____________________________________**
____.

Next, see how close you are to its meaning by consulting the list of definitions.

66. His 1960s long hair, sandals, and bushy beard were **anachronistic** and completely out of step with the current styles.

***How does this word get its meaning from its parts?*: (P5, Y17, W9)**

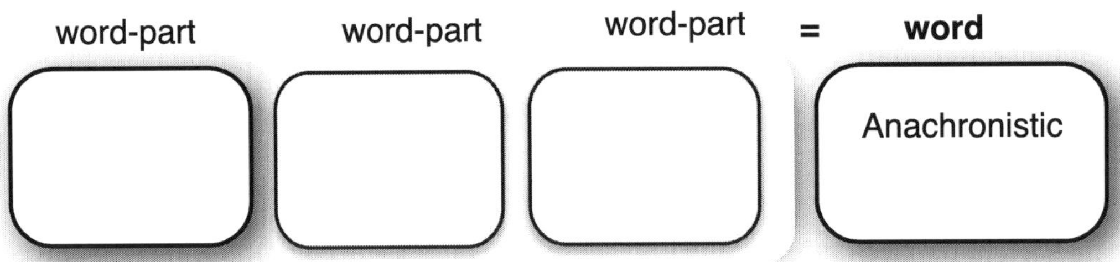

Considering the sentence context and these word-parts, what do you think this word means?
***I think that this word means*____________________________________**
____.

Next, see how close you are to its meaning by consulting the list of definitions.

Hints: P-Purple Cards,Y-Yellow Cards, B-Blue Cards, R-Red Cards, G-Green Cards, W-White Cards

67. It didn't matter what anyone told him: he was **adamant** about his belief that the world was flat.

***How does this word get its meaning from its parts?*: (P1, W34)**

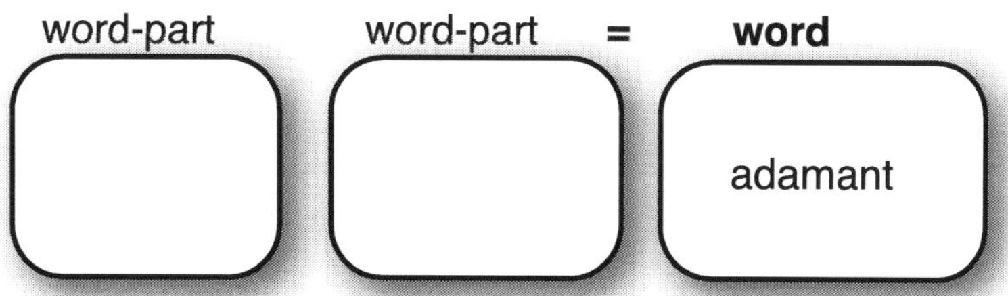

Considering the sentence context and these word-parts, what do you think this word means?
I think that this word means ____
____.

Next, see how close you are to its meaning by consulting the list of definitions.

68. No matter how hard she tried to **divert** attention from her pimples, everyone just kept staring at them.

***How does this word get its meaning from its parts?*:** (P13, G14)

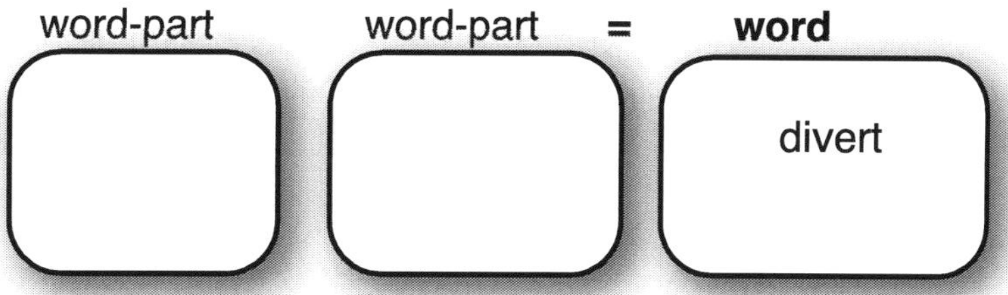

Considering the sentence context and these word-parts, what do you think this word means?
I think that this word means ____
____.

Next, see how close you are to its meaning by consulting the list of definitions.

Hints: P-Purple Cards,Y-Yellow Cards, B-Blue Cards, R-Red Cards, G-Green Cards, W-White Cards

69. His poor speaking ability **detracted** from his handsome appearance and turned his public performance into a disaster.

***How does this word get its meaning from its parts?*: (P11, G6)**

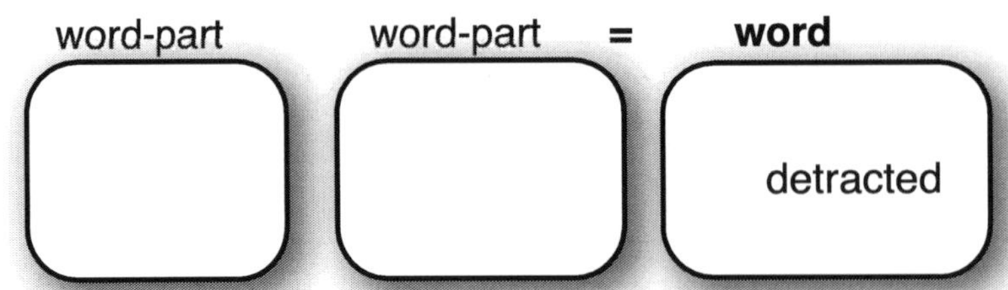

Considering the sentence context and these word-parts, what do you think this word means?
I think that this word means__________________________________
____.

Next, see how close you are to its meaning by consulting the list of definitions.

70. It was to his **discredit** that he never called his parents while they were sick.

***How does this word get its meaning from its parts?*: (P13, Y24)**

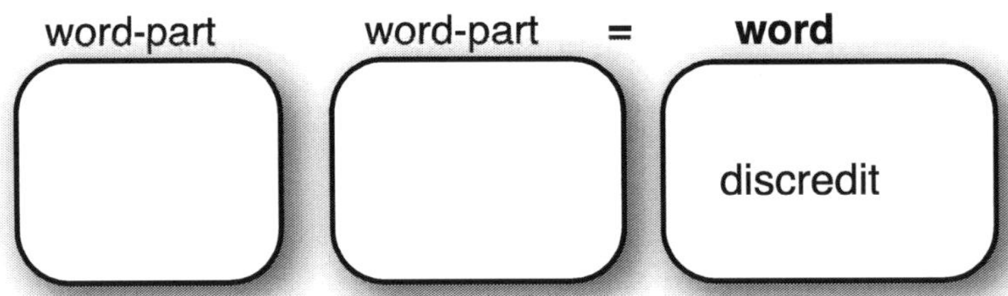

Considering the sentence context and these word-parts, what do you think this word means?
I think that this word means__________________________________
____.

Next, see how close you are to its meaning by consulting the list of definitions.

Hints: P-Purple Cards,Y-Yellow Cards, B-Blue Cards, R-Red Cards, G-Green Cards, W-White Cards

71. They seemed so **incompatible**; no one could believe that they were a match for each other. Yet, their marriage lasted for over fifty happy years.

***How does this word get its meaning from its parts?*: (P25, P10, W1)**

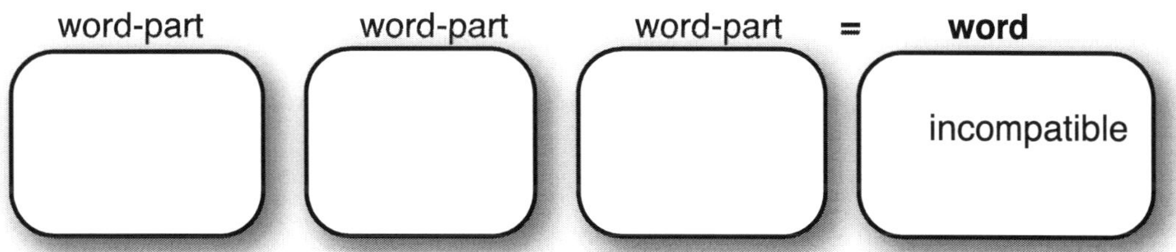

Considering the sentence context and these word-parts, what do you think this word means?
***I think that this word means*__________________________________**
____.

Next, see how close you are to its meaning by consulting the list of definitions.

72. The Southern states decided to **secede** from the Union, and they started a new nation known as the Confederacy.

***How does this word get its meaning from its parts?*: (B19, Y16)**

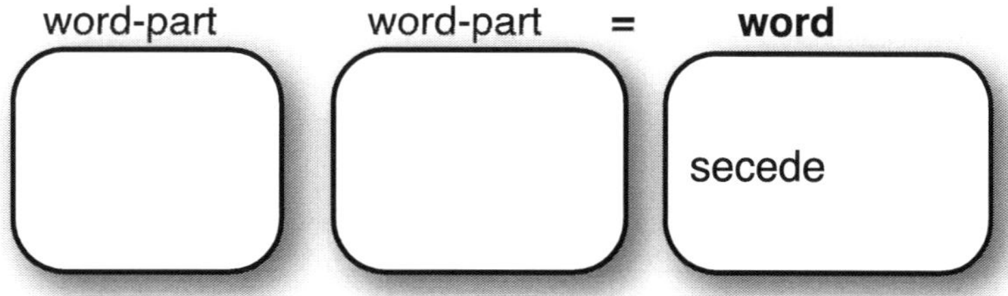

Considering the sentence context and these word-parts, what do you think this word means?
***I think that this word means*__________________________________**
____.

Next, see how close you are to its meaning by consulting the list of definitions.

Hints: P-Purple Cards,Y-Yellow Cards, B-Blue Cards, R-Red Cards, G-Green Cards, W-White Cards

73. Hip Hop music has added many **neologisms** to urban culture. For example, it has introduced the use of the word "mad" as an adverb to describe something that is truly wonderful: She was "mad" nice!

***How does this word get its meaning from its parts?*: (B1, R10)**

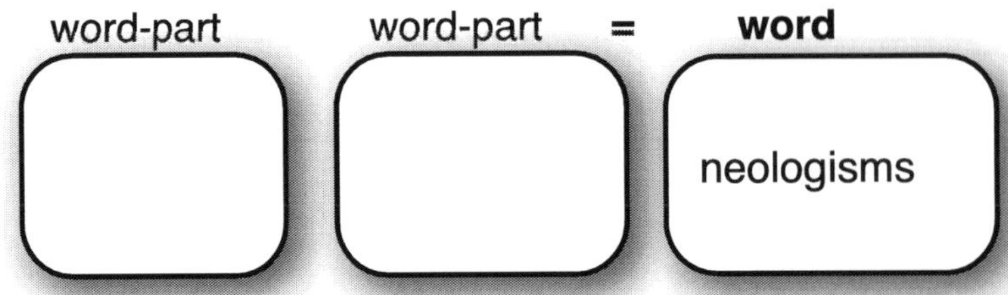

Considering the sentence context and these word-parts, what do you think this word means?
I think that this word means ____
____.

Next, see how close you are to its meaning by consulting the list of definitions.

74. The secretary complained that she was **inundated** with work. She said that she was drowning in emails and to-do lists.

***How does this word get its meaning from its parts?*: (P16, G8)**

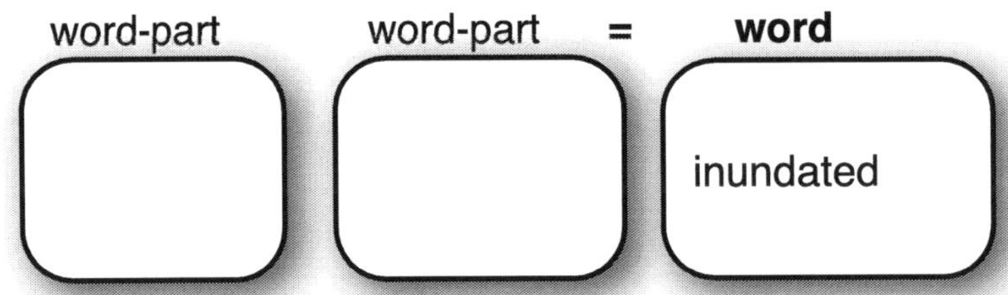

Considering the sentence context and these word-parts, what do you think this word means?
I think that this word means ____
____.

Next, see how close you are to its meaning by consulting the list of definitions.

Hints: P-Purple Cards,Y-Yellow Cards, B-Blue Cards, R-Red Cards, G-Green Cards, W-White Cards

75. **<u>Obsequiousness</u>** is defined as desiring to do anything to please someone.

***How does this word get its meaning from its parts?*: (P34, B21, W17)**

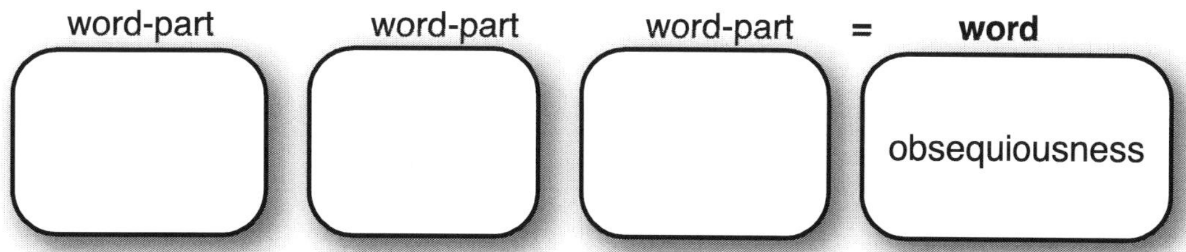

Considering the sentence context and these word-parts, what do you think this word means?
I think that this word means ______________________________
____.

Next, see how close you are to its meaning by consulting the list of definitions.

76. The **<u>interjection</u>** of commas between words in a list prevents the possibility of a run-on sentence.

***How does this word get its meaning from its parts?*: (P26, R9, W11)**

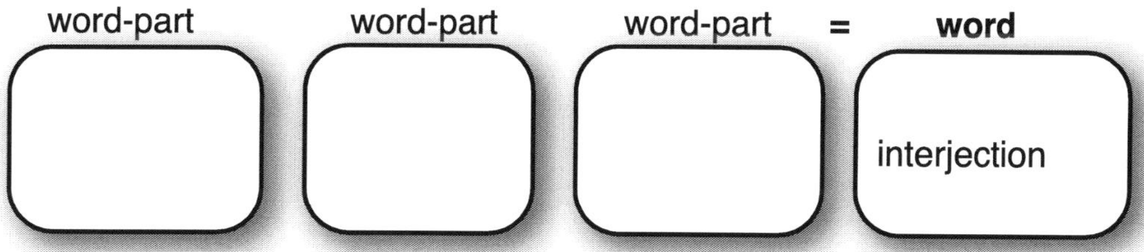

Considering the sentence context and these word-parts, what do you think this word means?
I think that this word means ______________________________
____.

Next, see how close you are to its meaning by consulting the list of definitions.

Hints: P-Purple Cards,Y-Yellow Cards, B-Blue Cards, R-Red Cards, G-Green Cards, W-White Cards

77. When I told him that his music was **euphonious**, he completely misunderstood me and thought that I was actually insulting him.

***How does this word get its meaning from its parts?*: (Y29, B10, W18)**

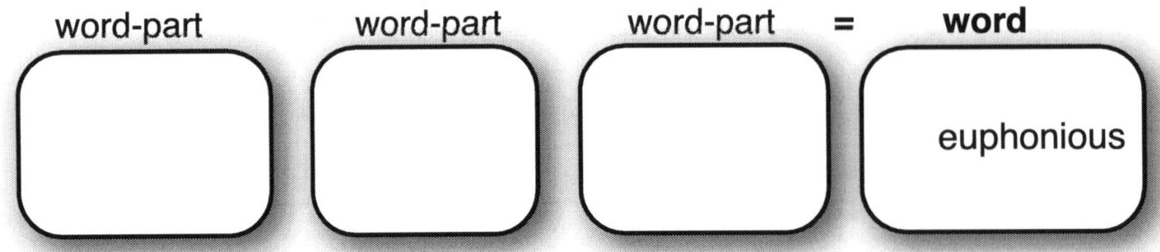

Considering the sentence context and these word-parts, what do you think this word means?
***I think that this word means*____**
____.

Next, see how close you are to its meaning by consulting the list of definitions.

78. Though they were behind for the entire game, the **pertinacious** team just would not quit, and they ended up winning the game.

***How does this word get its meaning from its parts?*: (P38, G3, W18)**

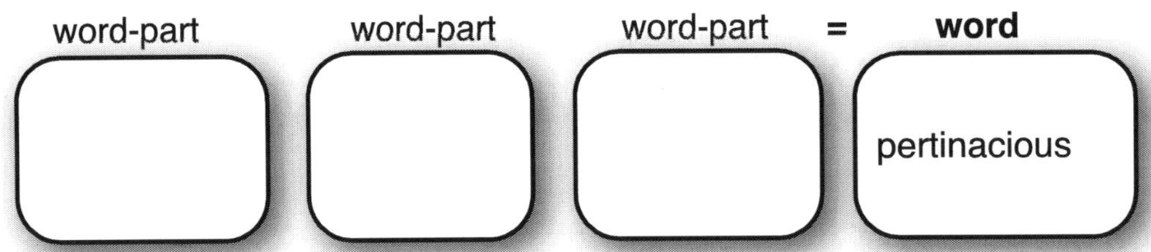

Considering the sentence context and these word-parts, what do you think this word means?
***I think that this word means*____**
____.

Next, see how close you are to its meaning by consulting the list of definitions.

Hints: P-Purple Cards,Y-Yellow Cards, B-Blue Cards, R-Red Cards, G-Green Cards, W-White Cards

79. No person should live in **subjection** to another: all men are created equal and should be equally free.

***How does this word get its meaning from its parts?*: (P45, R9, W11)**

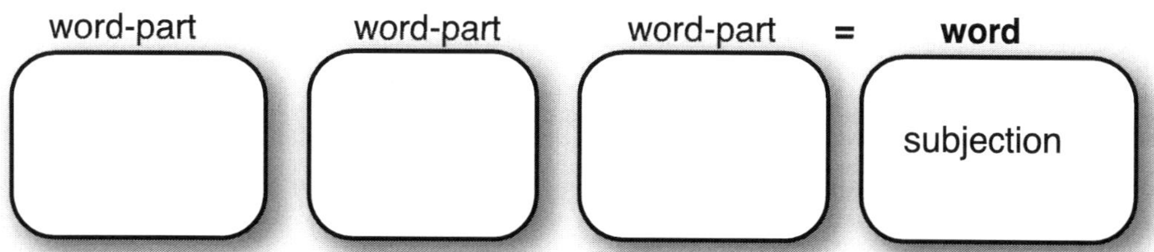

Considering the sentence context and these word-parts, what do you think this word means?
***I think that this word means*______________________________**

Next, see how close you are to its meaning by consulting the list of definitions.

80. During the **Reconstruction** era, the North helped to rebuild the South after the Civil War.

***How does this word get its meaning from its parts?*: (P43, P10, B28)**

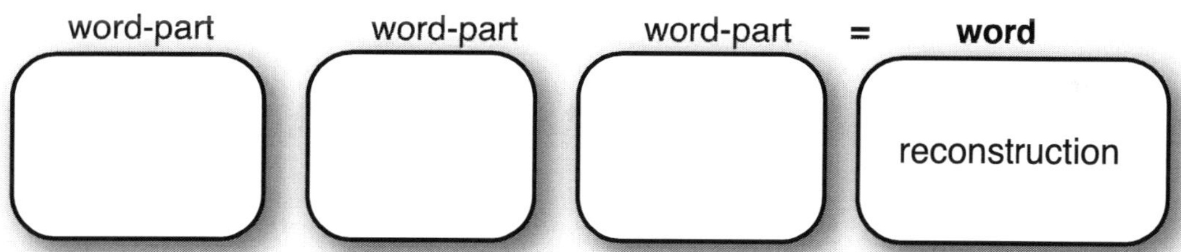

Considering the sentence context and these word-parts, what do you think this word means?
***I think that this word means*______________________________**
____.

Next, see how close you are to its meaning by consulting the list of definitions.

Hints: P-Purple Cards,Y-Yellow Cards, B-Blue Cards, R-Red Cards, G-Green Cards, W-White Cards

81. The United Nations was forced to i**<u>ntervene</u>** in order to prevent genocide.

***How does this word get its meaning from its parts?* (P26, G12)**

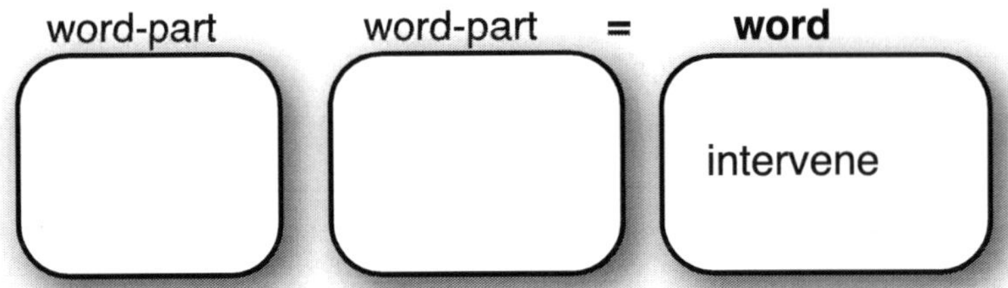

Considering the sentence context and these word-parts, what do you think this word means?
***I think that this word means*____**

____.

Next, see how close you are to its meaning by consulting the list of definitions.

82. The world has never recovered from the fear that came with the **<u>advent</u>** of the nuclear arms race.

***How does this word get its meaning from its parts?*: (P3, G12)**

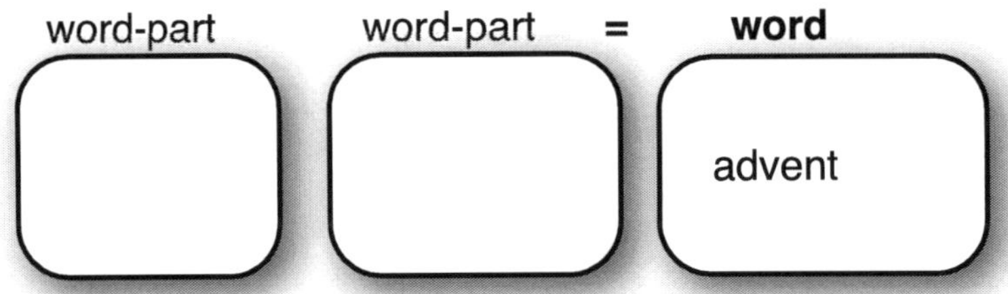

Considering the sentence context and these word-parts, what do you think this word means?
***I think that this word means*____**

____.

Next, see how close you are to its meaning by consulting the list of definitions.

Hints: P-Purple Cards,Y-Yellow Cards, B-Blue Cards, R-Red Cards, G-Green Cards, W-White Cards

83. The argument you made for not destroying the swamp simply to make way for the construction of a supermarket is both strong and **tenable**.

How does this word get its meaning from its parts?: **(G3, W1)**

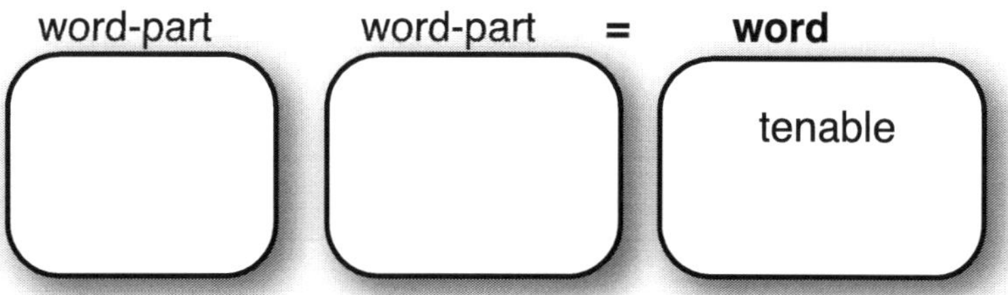

Considering the sentence context and these word-parts, what do you think this word means?
I think that this word means____________________________________
____.

Next, see how close you are to its meaning by consulting the list of definitions.

84. The evil king was warned that if he did not **abdicate** his power voluntarily, then it would be taken from him by force.

How does this word get its meaning from its parts?: **(P2, Y27)**

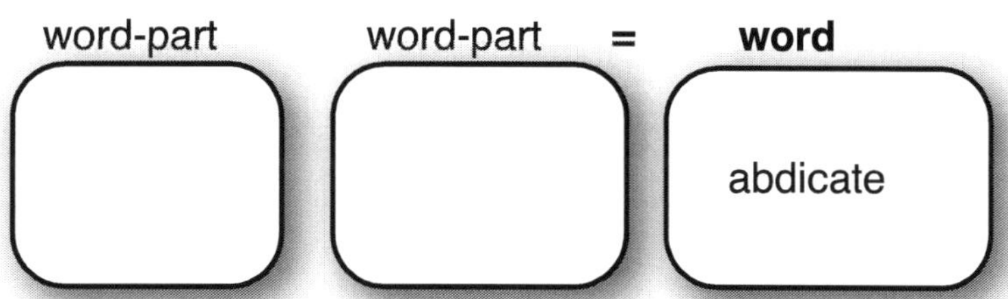

Considering the sentence context and these word-parts, what do you think this word means?
I think that this word means____________________________________
____.

Next, see how close you are to its meaning by consulting the list of definitions.

Hints: P-Purple Cards,Y-Yellow Cards, B-Blue Cards, R-Red Cards, G-Green Cards, W-White Cards

85. It is easy to make friends with **amicable** people.

***How does this word get its meaning from its parts?*: (Y2, W1)**

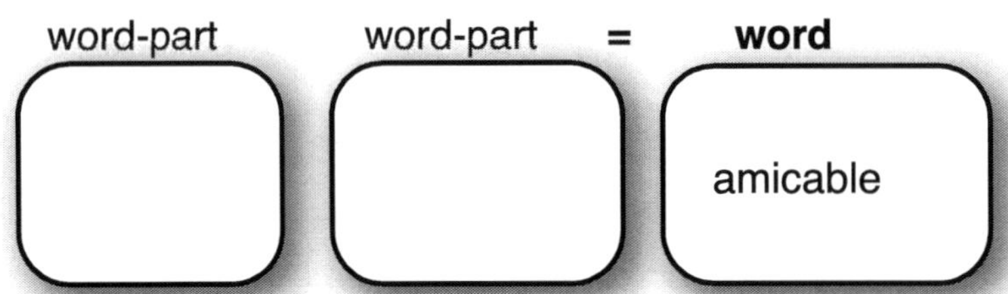

Considering the sentence context and these word-parts, what do you think this word means?
***I think that this word means*___________________________________**
____.

Next, see how close you are to its meaning by consulting the list of definitions.

86. Evan did not like the fact that people were **venerating** the league's best player. He did not think that an athlete was worthy of such respect.

***How does this word get its meaning from its parts?*: (G11, W10)**

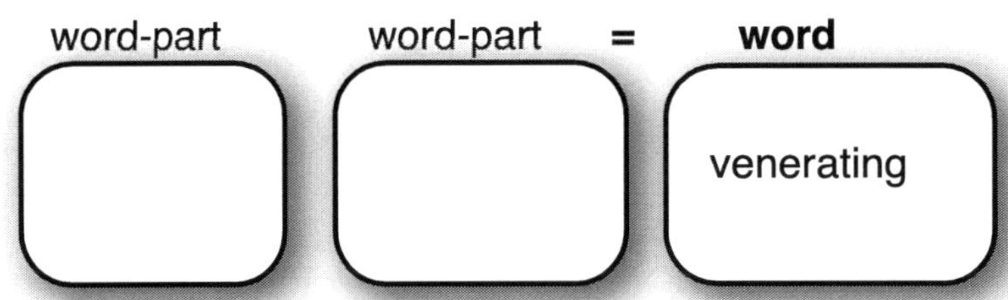

Considering the sentence context and these word-parts, what do you think this word means?
***I think that this word means*___________________________________**
____.

Next, see how close you are to its meaning by consulting the list of definitions.

Hints: P-Purple Cards,Y-Yellow Cards, B-Blue Cards, R-Red Cards, G-Green Cards, W-White Cards

87. It was only through power and force that he **acceded** to the throne.

***How does this word get its meaning from its parts?*: (P3, Y16)**

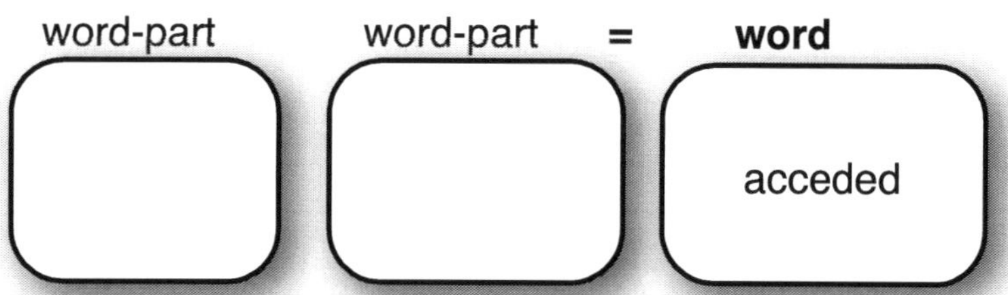

Considering the sentence context and these word-parts, what do you think this word means?
I think that this word means ______________________________
____.

Next, see how close you are to its meaning by consulting the list of definitions.

88. How could so many people be so **apathetic** and walk right by homeless strangers without seeming to have any feelings about their existence?

***How does this word get its meaning from its parts?*: (P1, W26)**

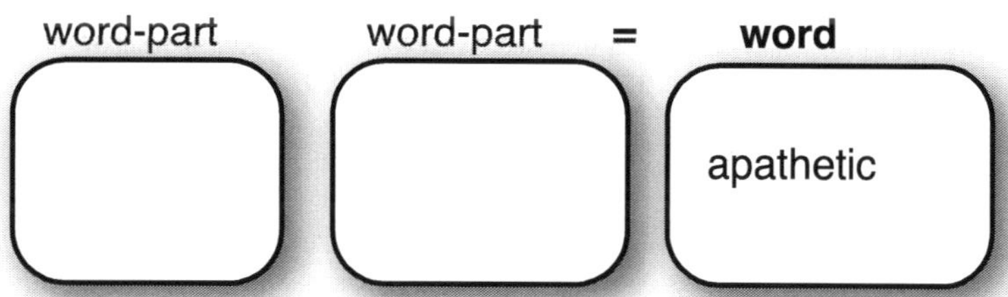

Considering the sentence context and these word-parts, what do you think this word means?
I think that this word means ______________________________
____.

Next, see how close you are to its meaning by consulting the list of definitions.

Hints: P-Purple Cards,Y-Yellow Cards, B-Blue Cards, R-Red Cards, G-Green Cards, W-White Cards

89. No one really knew who had committed the crime; all of their theories were just mere **conjectures** resulting from voicing their opinions instead of discussing the facts.

***How does this word get its meaning from its parts?*: (P10, R9)**

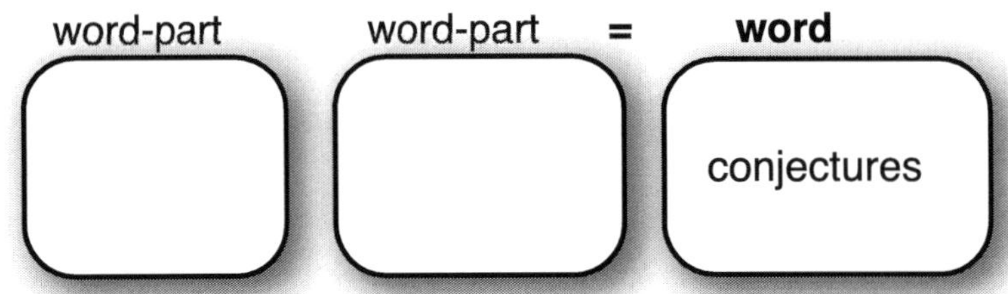

Considering the sentence context and these word-parts, what do you think this word means?

***I think that this word means*______________________________________**

____.

Next, see how close you are to its meaning by consulting the list of definitions.

90. Mary's teacher gave her an **incredulous** look when she heard Mary's tale that the dog had eaten her homework.

***How does this word get its meaning from its parts?*: (P25, Y24, W18)**

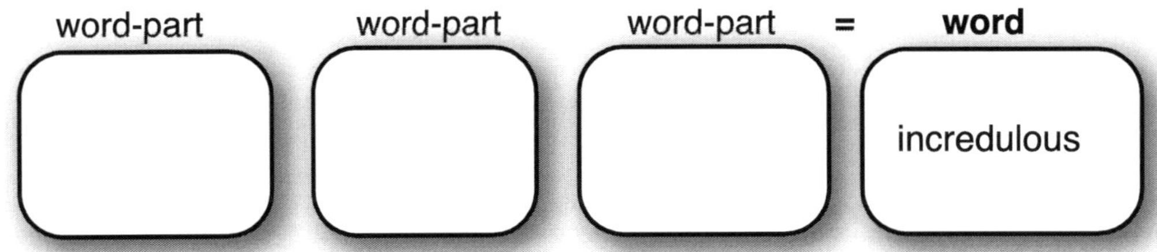

Considering the sentence context and these word-parts, what do you think this word means?

***I think that this word means*______________________________________**

____.

Next, see how close you are to its meaning by consulting the list of definitions.

Hints: P-Purple Cards,Y-Yellow Cards, B-Blue Cards, R-Red Cards, G-Green Cards, W-White Cards

91. The researchers warned that the destruction of the rain forests and the **concomitant** extinction of species would cause irreversible harm to the earth.

***How does this word get its meaning from its parts?*: (P10, Y19)**

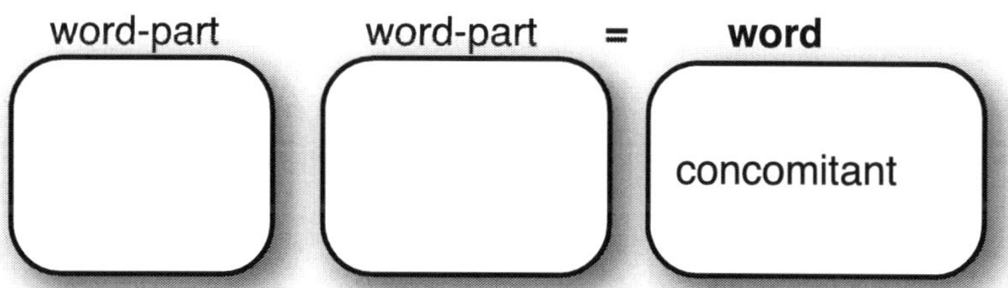

Considering the sentence context and these word-parts, what do you think this word means?
I think that this word means____
____.

Next, see how close you are to its meaning by consulting the list of definitions.

92. No one should try to say any words of comfort to the grieving without first trying to **empathize** with them and truly understand their feelings.

***How does this word get its meaning from its parts?*: (P16, W26)**

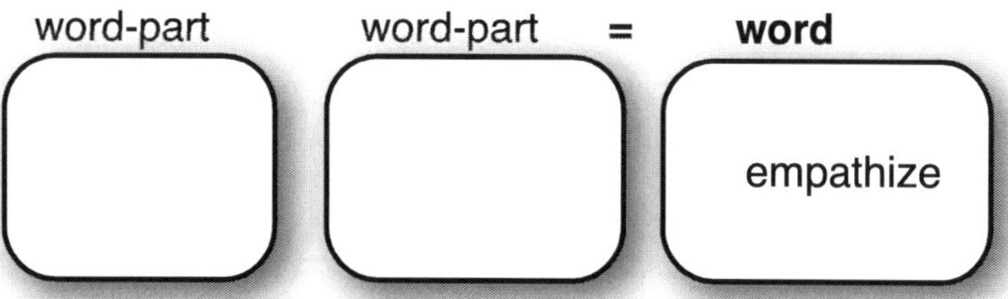

Considering the sentence context and these word-parts, what do you think this word means?
I think that this word means____
____.

Next, see how close you are to its meaning by consulting the list of definitions.

Hints: P-Purple Cards,Y-Yellow Cards, B-Blue Cards, R-Red Cards, G-Green Cards, W-White Cards

93. The billionaire showed his **benevolence** by donating large sums of money to the poor and the underprivileged. He was truly a **philanthropist**.

***How does the first word get its meaning from its parts?*: (Y11, G15)**

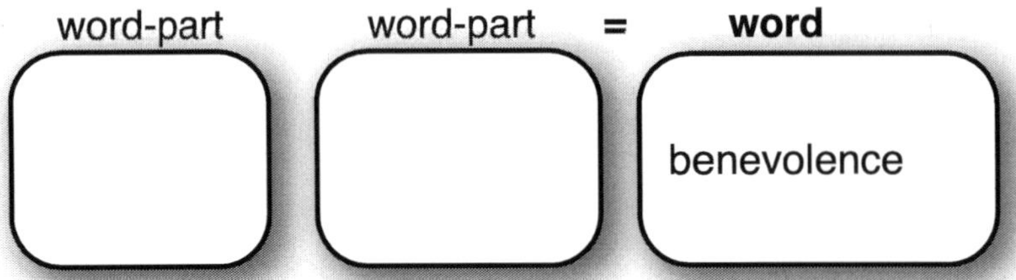

Considering the sentence context and these word-parts, what do you think this word means?
***I think that this word means*____**
____.

Next, see how close you are to its meaning by consulting the list of definitions.

***How does the second word get its meanings from its parts:* (B8, Y7, W22)**

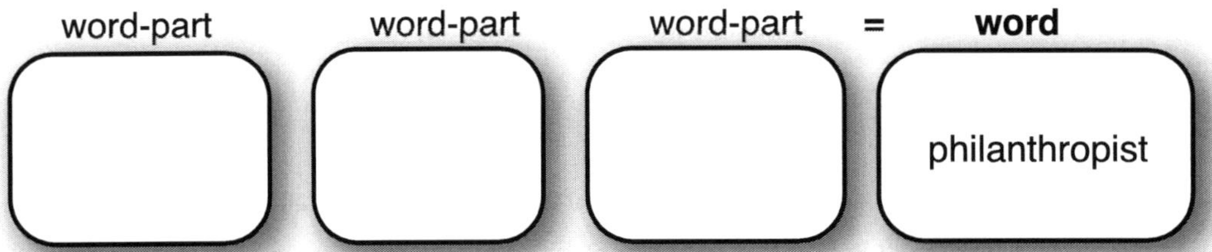

Considering the sentence context and these word-parts, what do you think this word means?
***I think that this word means*____**
____.

Next, see how close you are to its meaning by consulting the list of definitions.

Hints: P-Purple Cards,Y-Yellow Cards, B-Blue Cards, R-Red Cards, G-Green Cards, W-White Cards

94. Several people **<u>conspired</u>** to kill the president; fortunately for him, their plans were intercepted.

***How does the first word get its meaning from its parts?*: (P10, B26)**

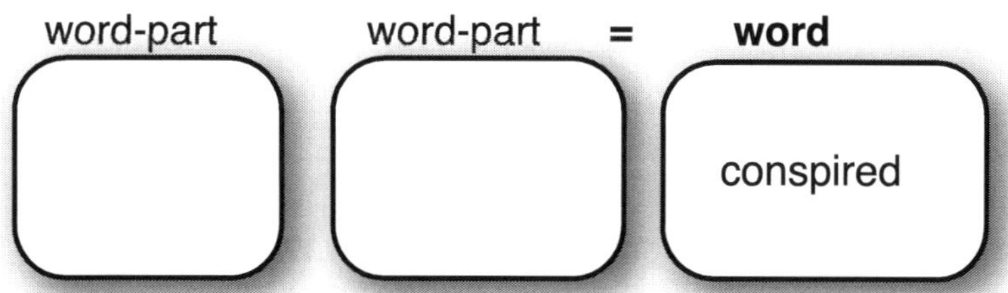

Considering the sentence context and these word-parts, what do you think this word means?
I think that this word means ______________________________________

____.

Next, see how close you are to its meaning by consulting the list of definitions.

95. Because he had pronounced **<u>maledictions</u>** against them instead of the blessings they desired, the villagers tried to throw their old religious leader out of the village.

***How does the word get its meaning from its parts?*: (P28, Y27)**

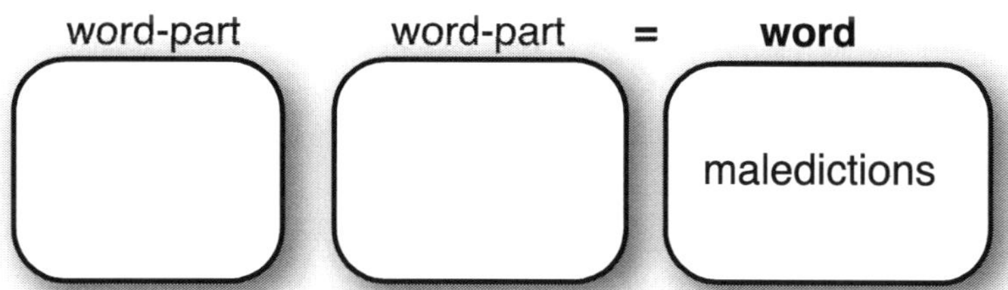

Considering the sentence context and these word-parts, what do you think this word means?
I think that this word means ______________________________________

____.

Next, see how close you are to its meaning by consulting the list of definitions.

Hints: P-Purple Cards,Y-Yellow Cards, B-Blue Cards, R-Red Cards, G-Green Cards, W-White Cards

96. The multimillionaire became a **benefactor** to many poor young people by giving them scholarships for college.

***How does the word get its meaning from its parts?*: (Y11, Y30)**

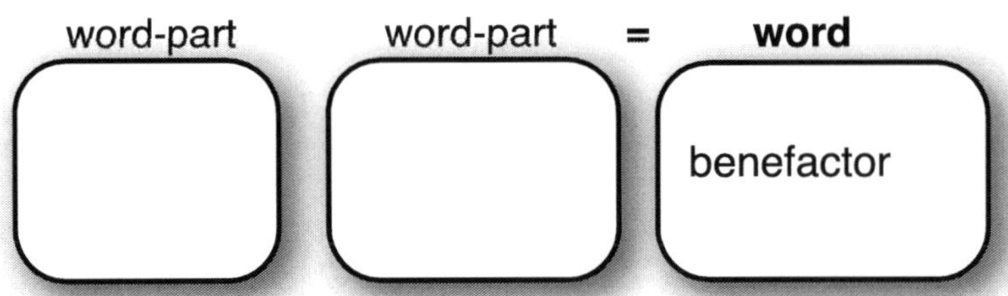

Considering the sentence context and these word-parts, what do you think this word means?
I think that this word means ____
____.

Next, see how close you are to its meaning by consulting the list of definitions.

97. Because the politician's campaign was failing, he decided to unleash a storm of **obloquy** against his opponent. He began trying to discredit him with all forms of abusive language and harsh criticisms.

***How does the word get its meaning from its parts?*: (P34, R12)**

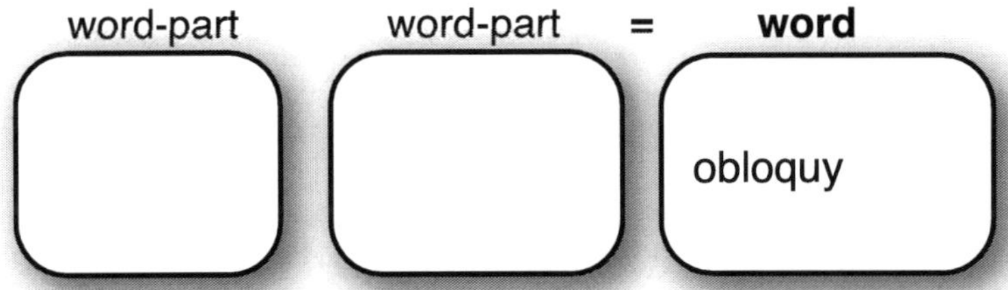

Considering the sentence context and these word-parts, what do you think this word means?
I think that this word means ____
____.

Next, see how close you are to its meaning by consulting the list of definitions.

Hints: P-Purple Cards,Y-Yellow Cards, B-Blue Cards, R-Red Cards, G-Green Cards, W-White Cards

98. He was rude and crude, and his **despicable** behavior caused everyone to look down upon him.

***How does the word get its meaning from its parts?*: (P11, B25)**

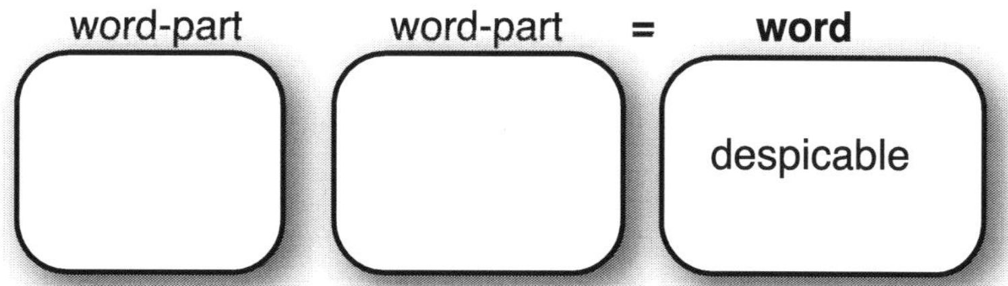

Considering the sentence context and these word-parts, what do you think this word means?
I think that this word means____
____.

Next, see how close you are to its meaning by consulting the list of definitions.

99. Most students prefer **synchronous** online classes where the teacher and the student are present at the same time.

***How does the word get its meaning from its parts?*: (P47, Y17)**

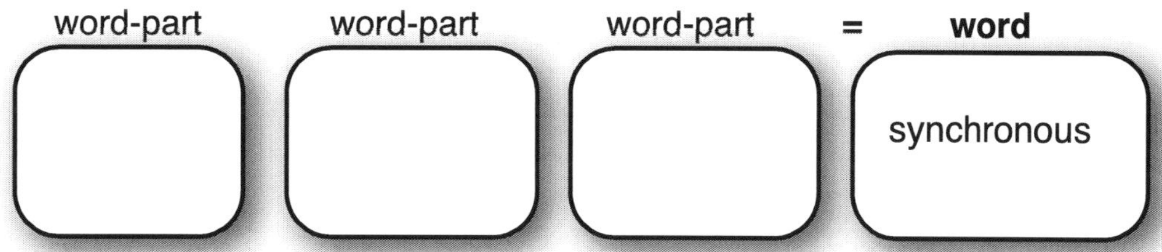

Considering the sentence context and these word-parts, what do you think this word means?
I think that this word means____
____.

Next, see how close you are to its meaning by consulting the list of definitions.

Hints: P-Purple Cards,Y-Yellow Cards, B-Blue Cards, R-Red Cards, G-Green Cards, W-White Cards

100. Politicians often try to **circumvent** the real issues, instead of dealing with them in a direct and straightforward manner.

***How does the word get its meaning from its parts?*: (Y18, G12)**

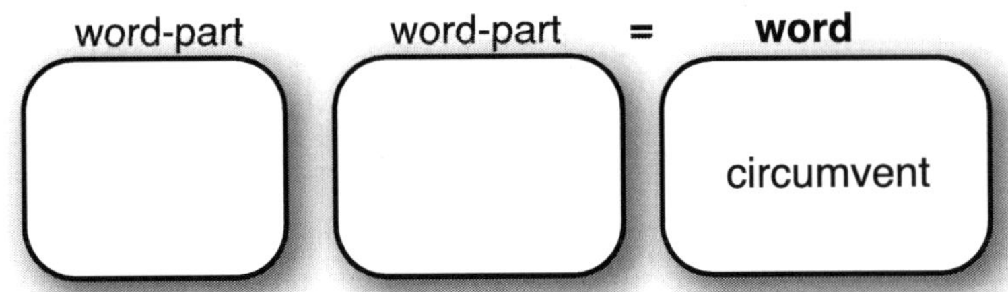

Considering the sentence context and these word-parts, what do you think this word means?
***I think that this word means*____**
____.

Next, see how close you are to its meaning by consulting the list of definitions.

Hints: P-Purple Cards,Y-Yellow Cards, B-Blue Cards, R-Red Cards, G-Green Cards, W-White Cards

Appendix A
Review and Extra Derivative Words

Hints: P-Purple Cards,Y-Yellow Cards, B-Blue Cards, R-Red Cards, G-Green Cards, W-White Cards

Definitions of Vocabulary Words Used in Sentences Word List One

1. **Abdicate:** (v.) to give up a position, right, or power; to disown
2. **Abstain:** (v.) to hold back, refrain (especially from something bad or unhealthy); to choose not to do something
3. **Accede:** (v.) to agree to; to yield to; to assume an office or dignity
4. **Accord:** (n.) agreement, harmony
   (v.) to agree; to be in harmony or bring into harmony; to grant, bestow on
5. **Adamant:** (adj.) firm in purpose or opinion, unyielding, obdurate, implacable, inflexible, stubborn
6. **Advent:** 1. arrival or coming into being 2. (capitalized) The period beginning four weeks before Christmas; the birth of Christ
7. **Amateur:** (n.) person who does something for pleasure, not for money as a profession; a beginner, not a professional
   (adj.) lacking professional skill or expertise.
8. **Amiable:** (adj.) friendly, good-natured; pleasant, likable
9. **Amicable:** (adj.) friendly
10. **Anachronism:** (n.) something out of place in time
11. **Anarchy:** (n) a lack of government and law; confusion; disorder
12. **Antebellum:** (adj.) belonging to a period before a war, especially the American Civil War
13. **Antipathy:** (adj.) hatred; strong dislike
14. **Apathetic:** (adj.) feeling or showing little emotion; indifferent
15. **Aspire:** (v.) to have ambitious hopes or plans, strive toward a higher goal, desire earnestly; to ascend
16. **Atheist:** (n.) a person who does not believe in God
17. **Autocracy:** (n.) a system of government in which the power to rule is in the hands of a single individual
18. **Benefactor:** One who does good to others
19. **Benevolent:** (adj.) kind; favorable; generous
20. **Bibliophile:** (n.) one who loves books
21. **Catastrophe:** (n.) a large-scale disaster, misfortune, or failure; an event resulting in great loss and misfortune
22. **Chronometer:** (n.) a timepiece; a watch; a clock; a device used to measure time
23. **Circumlocution:** (n.) an indirect way of expressing something; evasive or roundabout speech
24. **Circumscribe:** (v.) to draw a circle around; to restrict, limit
25. **Circumspect:** (adj.) careful, cautious
26. **Circumstantial:** (adj.; incidental; indirect
27. **Circumvent:** To circle AROUND and therefore bypass; to avoid by artful maneuvering;
   (v.) to get around (The school's dress code forbidding navel-baring jeans was circumvented by the determined students, who were careful to cover up with long coats when administrators were nearby.)
28. **Concomitant:** (adj.) accompanying in a subordinate fashion; following as a consequence
29. **Concord:** (n.) a state of agreement, harmony, unanimity; a treaty, pact, covenant
30. **Congenital:** (adj.) existing at birth
31. **Conjecture:** (n.) an inference based upon guesswork; a supposition
32. **Consequence:** (n.) a result or effect of an action or condition.
33. **conspicuous: (adj.) easy to see or understand**
34. **Conspire:** (v.) to plan together secretly to do something wrong or illegal
35. **Contemporaneous:** (adj.) happening at or around the same time
36. **Contradict:** (v.) to speak against; to say the opposite; to disagree
37. **Contravene:** (v.) to contradict, deny, act contrary to; to go against
38. **Convene:** (v.) to assemble, especially for a meeting; to call together
39. **Convert:** (v.) to change
40. **Dejected:** (adj.) downcast or sad; depressed
41. **Despicable:** (adj.) worthy of scorn, contemptible, worthy of being looked down upon
42. **Detain:** (v.) to delay; to stop or hold; to keep from going on
43. **Detract:** (v.) to take away from; reduce in value or reputation
44. **Discord:** (adj.) disagreeable in sound, jarring; lacking in harmony, conflicting
   (n.) a harsh, dissonant sound; conflict; disagreement
45. **Discredit:** (v.) to dishonor, disgrace; to destroy the reputation of
46. **Disinformation:** (n.) false information purposely disseminated, usually by a government, for the purpose of creating a false impression
47. **Disseminate:** (v.) to scatter or spread widely
48. **Distend:** (v.) to swell, inflate, or bloat; to expand
49. **Divert:** (v.) to turn aside from a course or direction; to draw away attention
50. **Dystopian:** (n.) a futuristic society that seems perfect, but really is not; an imaginary bad place, usually refers to a vision of the future
   (adj.) nightmarish, grim
51. **Edict:** (n.) an official order issued by someone in authority
52. **Egregious:** (adj.) conspicuously bad or offensive
53. **Emerge:** (v.) to come out into view, as from concealment; to come into sight
54. **Empathetic:** (n.) identifying with and understanding another's situation, feelings, and motives; feeling another's pain as one's own
55. **Encomium:** (n.) glowing and enthusiastic praise; panergyric, tribute, eulogy
56. **Euphonious:** (adj.) having a pleasant and melodious sound
57. **Expire:** (v.) to come to an end; to die
58. **Explicate:** (v.) to make plain or clear, explain; to interpret
59. **Extrovert:** (n.) an outgoing and sociable person
   (adj.) having an outgoing personality
60. **Implicate:** (v.) to involve in; to connect with or be related to
61. **incomparable:** (n.) not capable of being compared; incapable of being equaled; matchless
62. **Incompatible:** (adj.) opposed in nature, not able to live or work together; not harmonious
63. **Inconceivable:** (adj.) impossible to believe or imagine; hard to fully grasp or comprehend
64. **Incontrovertible:** (adj.) indisputable; beyond doubt
65. **Incorporate:** (v.) to bring together features, ideas, or elements; to combine

66. **Incredulous:** (adj.) showing disbelief, skeptical
67. **Indestructible:** (adj.) not capable of being destroyed
68. **Inseminate:** (v.) to implant semen into (a female), to sow; implant seed, to sow new ideas, implant into the mind
69. **Insemination:** (n.) process of introducing semen into the uterus or tubes of a woman
70. **Inspire:** (v.) to fill with emotion or great excitement
71. **Insuperable:** (adj.) incapable of being overcome or defeated; insurmountable
72. **Interception:** (n.) In football, the act of catching a football thrown by a player on the opposing team; unauthorized access of information (e.g. tapping, sniffing, unsecured wireless communication, emanations)
73. **interjection:** (n.) A word that expresses strong feeling or emotion, A word thrown into a sentence or conversation
74. **Intervene:** (v)To come between in order to influence an action, an argument, etc., to come between opposing groups; to mediate; to take place; to occur between time
75. **Intractable:** (adj.) not easily managed or directed; hard to tame or control; stubborn, obstinate
76. **Intransigent:** (adj.) refusing to compromise, irreconcilable
77. **Introspective:** (adj.) contemplating one's own thoughts and feelings; looking inwards
78. **Inundate:** (v.) to flood, overflow; to overwhelm by numbers or size
79. **Invincible:** (adj.) not able to be defeated, unbeatable
80. **Loquacious:** (adj.) talkative
81. **Maledictions:** Curses;
word/phrase uttered with intent to bring about evil, curse
82. **Malevolent:** (adj.) spiteful, showing ill will; desiring to to bad things and hurt others
83. **Manuscript:** (n.) a handwritten document
84. **Misanthropy:** (n.) hatred of humanity
85. **Misperception:** (n.) an incorrect understanding of something; a misunderstanding; a flawed conclusion
86. **Monarchy:** (n.) a government ruled by a king or queen; a government in which power is in the hands of a single person
87. **Monotheistic:** (adj.) believing in one god
88. **Neologism:** (n.) new word or expression
89. **Obdurate:** (adj.) stubborn, unyielding
90. **Object:** (v.) to speak out against something
91. **Obloquy:** censure, blame, or abusive language aimed at a person or thing, especially by numerous persons or by the general public; disgrace or discredit from public blame.
92. **Obsequious:** (adj.) acting like a servant; servile
93. **Omnipotent:** (adj.) all-powerful
94. **Omniscience:** (n.) infinite knowledge; the state of knowing everything
95. **Overextended:** (adj.) going beyond a safe, reasonable point; always doing something (maybe too much)
96. **Pedometer:** (n.) a device that calculates distance traveled by walking
97. **Perambulate:** (v.) to walk about; to stroll; to stroll, wander
98. **Perceive:** (v.) to understand, know, become aware of
99. **Periscope:** (n.) instrument permitting those in a submarine a view of the surface
100. **Permit:** (v.) to allow
101. **Perspicacious:** (adj.) keen; mentally sharp; acute; shrewd
102. **Pertinacious:** (adj.) very persistent; holding firmly to a course of action or a set of beliefs; hard to get rid of, refusing to be put off or denied
103. **Philanthropy:** (n.) charity; a desire or effort to promote goodness; love of mankind
104. **Polytheist:** (n.) one who believes in many gods
105. **Precipice:** (n.) literally head first, a steep face of a rock, a fall or a leap, on the brink of danger
106. **Prescience:** (n.) foreknowledge of events; knowing of events prior to their occurring; foresight
107. **Projectile:** (n.) an object thrown into the air with great force
108. **Proscribe:** (v) prohibit, outlaw; denounce; exile or banish
109. **Recede:** (v.) to go or move backward; to become more distant
110. **Reconstruction:** (n; history) 1865-1877; the attempt to rebuild and reform the political, social, and economic systems of the South after the Civil War.
(n.) the act or process of rebuilding something
111. **Redundant:** (adj.) extra, excess, more than is needed; wordy, needlessly repetitive; profuse, lush;
112. **Regenerative:** (adj.) growing back; becoming new
113. **Remit:** (v.) to send or hand in (as money); to cancel (as a penalty or punishment), forgive, pardon; to lessen, diminish; to put off, postpone, defer
114. **Renascent:** (adj.) acquiring or showing new life, strength, or vigor; reborn
115. **Resegregate:** (v.) to separate groups of people again
116. **Respire:** (v.) to breathe
117. **Restructure:** (v.) construct or form anew; to provide with a new structure
118. **Retain:** (v.) to hold or keep
119. **Retention:** (n) ability to recall or recognize things learned or experienced; preservation; withholding
120. **Reticent:** (adj.) silent; reserved; not talking much
121. **Retrospect:** (adj.) looking back
(n.) a survey of past times or events; hindsight
122. **Secede:** (v.) to leave or withdraw; to break away
123. **Seduce:** (v.) to lure or entice away from duty, principles, or proper conduct
124. **Segregate:** (v.) to separate or keep apart from others
125. **Subconscious:** (adj.) not fully aware; occurring below your level of thinking and awareness
126. **Subjection:** (n.) the conquering of or bringing under control of; dependence, obedience, submission
127. **Submerge:** (v.) to fill or cover completely, usually with water; to go underwater
128. **Subservient:** (adj.) subordinate in capacity or role; submissively obedient; serving to promote some end; acting like a servant
129. **Subterranean:** (adj.) underground; beneath the surface of the Earth
130. **Susceptible:** (adj.) open to; easily influenced; lacking in resistance
131. **Suspire:** (v.) to breath; to sigh

132. **Sustain:** (v.) to support, nourish, keep up; to suffer, undergo; to bear up under, withstand; to affirm the validity of

133. **Synchronize:** to occur at the same time; simultaneous

134. **Tenable:** (adj.) capable of being held or defended

135. **Tenacious:** (adj) holding fast; holding together firmly; persistent

136. **Theocracy:** (n.) a form of government where God, or a god, is recognized as the civil ruler of a state, and where religious authorities rule the state as God's, or the god's, representatives

137. **Transient:** (adj.) lasting only a short time, fleeting
(n.) one who stays only a short time

138. **Unambiguous:** (adj.) clear, distinct, definite, precise

139. **Unequivocal:** (adj.) absolute; certain; clear; obvious

140. **Untenable:** (adj.) not capable of being held or defended; impossible to maintain

141. **Venerable:** (adj.) commanding or deserving respect

142. **Venerate:** (v.) to regard with reverence, look up to with great respect; to respect deeply

ScholarSkills Vocabulary Word List 2

Study online at quizlet.com/_2gmt20

1.	**Abduct**	(v.) to kidnap
2.	**Abject**	(adj.) degraded; base, contemptible; cringing, servile; complete and unrelieved; miserable, pitiful
3.	**Abrupt**	(adj.) brief and sudden
4.	**Abstain**	(v.) to choose not to do something; to hold back, deny oneself
5.	**Abstract**	(adj.) difficult to understand
6.	**Abstruse**	(adj.) difficult to understand
7.	**Accede**	(v.) to agree with; to yield to; to assume an office or dignity
8.	**Adherent**	(n.) a follower, supporter (adj.) attached, sticking to
9.	**Advent**	(n.) an arrival; a coming into place or view
10.	**adverse**	(adj) unfavorable, negative; working against, hostile
11.	**Aggregate**	(adj.) gathered into a whole; total
12.	**Ascend**	(v.) to rise or go up
13.	**Ascribe**	(v.) to assign or refer to (as a cause or source)
14.	**Aspect**	(n.) a part that can be considered or viewed; a trait or characteristic
15.	**Aspire**	(v.) to have ambitious hopes or plans; strive toward a higher goal; desire earnestly; to ascend
16.	**Assiduous**	(adj.) diligent, hardworking; persistent
17.	**Attract**	(v.) to cause to draw near by some quality or action; to pull toward one another
18.	**Chronograph**	(n.) a device to measure and record time
19.	**Circumcision**	(n.) removal of the foreskin
20.	**Circumlocution**	(adj.) evasive speech; the act of talking around a topic
21.	**Circumscribe**	(v.) to draw a circle around; to limit or restrict
22.	**Circumspect**	(adj.) careful, cautious
23.	**Circumvent**	(v.) to circle AROUND and therefore bypass; to avoid by artful maneuvering; to avoid
24.	**Coherent**	(adj.) holding or sticking together; logically connected; comprehensible, meaningful
25.	**Colloquial**	(adj.) characteristic of ordinary conversation rather than formal speech or writing
26.	**Commit**	(v.) to pledge; to do or perform; to entrust
27.	**Compartment**	(n.) a separate room or section
28.	**Compel**	(v.) to force
29.	**Complicate**	(v.) to make difficult to understand
30.	**Compress**	(v.) to press together; force into less space; to shorten or abbreviate
31.	**Concede**	(v.) to admit as true; to yield, submit; to acknowledge
32.	**Conceive**	(v.) to come up with, imagine; to understand
33.	**Concise**	(adj.) brief, to the point
34.	**Concur**	(v.) to agree
35.	**Conduct**	(n.) behavior; way of acting (v.) to act or behave in a certain way
36.	**Confer**	(v.) to consult, talk over, exchange opinions; to present as a gift, favor, or honor
37.	**Conform**	(v.) to change or adjust one's behavior or thinking to coincide with a group standard.
38.	**Congregation**	(n.) a crowd of people, an assembly
39.	**Conjecture**	(n.) an educated guess based on observations
40.	**Consist**	(v.) to be made up of
41.	**Conspire**	(v.) to plan together secretly to do something wrong or illegal
42.	**Construct**	(v.) to build
43.	**Contort**	(v.) to twist or bend out of shape
44.	**Convene**	(v.) to come or call together; to assemble, especially for a meeting
45.	**Converse**	(v.) to chat; talk informally (n.) formal talk
46.	**Convivial**	(adj.) festive, sociable, having fun together, genial
47.	**Convocation**	(n.) a group united for a particular purpose; an assembly
48.	**Convoluted**	(adj.) hard to understand; complex or complicated
49.	**Deactivate**	(v.) to make inactive or unable to work
50.	**decelerate**	(v.) to slow down or to cause to slow down
51.	**Decisive**	(adj.) conclusive; beyond doubt; unmistakable; certain
52.	**Defect**	(n.) An imperfection, flaw, or blemish of some kind (v.) to desert a cause or organization; to betray
53.	**Deform**	(v.) to damage the natural form or shape of; put out of shape; disfigure
54.	**Dejected**	(adj.) sad or depressed
55.	**Denounce**	(v.) to condemn, criticize
56.	**Depleted**	(adj.) emptied; drained; used up
57.	**Desist**	(v.) to stop
58.	**Destructive**	(adj.) harmful; dangerous
59.	**Detract**	(v.) to diminsh; to take away from; reduce in value or reputation
60.	**Devise**	(v.) to think out, plan, figure out, invent, create
61.	**Devolve**	(v.) to grow worse; to bring to a lower level

62.	**Diagraph**	(n.) an instrument for enlarging or projecting drawings
63.	**Digraph**	Two letters that represent one sound. There are consonant digraphs and vowel digraphs, such as "sh, ch, th, wh, ew, aw, oo"
64.	**Dispel**	(v.) to drive away
65.	**Disrupt**	(v.) to destroy; to cause disorder; to break apart
66.	**Dissuade**	(v.) to persuade not to do something
67.	**Distend**	(v.) to swell, inflate, expand, or bloat
68.	**Distort**	(v.) to give a false or misleading account of; to twist out of shape
69.	**Divert**	(v.) to turn aside from a course or direction
70.	**Division**	(n.) separation
71.	**Edict**	(n.) an order issued by someone in authority; a decree or proclamation
72.	**Egregious**	(adj.) conspicuously bad; standing out from the mass (used particularly in an unfavorable sense)
73.	**Elocution**	(n.) the art of public speaking
74.	**Eloquent**	(adj.) fluent or persuasive in speaking or writing.
75.	**Emerge**	(v.) to rise up or come forth; to come into view
76.	**Emit**	(v.) to send out; to give off
77.	**Endemic**	(adj.) native or confined to a particular region or people
78.	**Epidemic**	(n.) a widespread outbreak of an infectious disease.
79.	**Epigraph**	(n.) a brief quotation found at the beginning of a literary work, reflective of theme.
80.	**Erupt**	(v.) to burst forth, break out
81.	**Evade**	(v.) to elude or avoid by being smart or cunning; to flee from a pursuer.
82.	**Evoke**	(v.) to summon or call forth
83.	**Evolve**	(v.) to develop gradually; to rise to a higher level
84.	**Exceed**	(v.) to do or go beyond; to surpass
85.	**Excise**	(v.) to cut out of; remove
86.	**Excite**	(v.) to arouse or stir up the emotions or feelings of; to provoke to action
87.	**Exclude**	(v.) to leave or keep out
88.	**Excursion**	(n.) a trip or outing for means of pleasure
89.	**Expel**	(v.) to force or drive out
90.	**Expire**	(v.) to come to an end; to die
91.	**Explicate**	(v.) to make plain or clear, explain; to interpret
92.	**Extort**	(v.) to obtain by violence, misuse of authority, or threats; to blackmail
93.	**Immerse**	(v.) to plunge or dip into a fluid; to involve deeply
94.	**Impart**	(v.) to tell or make known
95.	**Impel**	(v) to force, drive forward; to push into motion
96.	**Implicate**	(v.) to involve in; to connect with or be related to
97.	**Inadvertently**	(adv.) accidentally
98.	**Incite**	(v.) to arouse to action; to stir up; urge on
99.	**Incur**	(v.) to bring about; to meet with; to run into; to bring upon oneself
100.	**induce**	(v.) to cause, bring about; to persuade
101.	**Induct**	(v.) to introduce or install
102.	**Inherent**	(adj.) firmly established by nature or habit
103.	**Inscribe**	(v.) to write or engrave; to enter a name on a list
104.	**Instruct**	(v.) to teach
105.	**Intercede**	(v.) to plead on behalf of someone else; to serve as a third party or go-between in a disagreement
106.	**Intercept**	(v.) to take away; obstruct
107.	**Interject**	(v.) to put between other things
108.	**Interlocution**	(n.) conversation between two or more people
109.	**Intermittent**	(adj.) stopping and beginning again; sporadic
110.	**Intervene**	(v.) to come in between
111.	**Intrude**	(v.) to come or go in without permission or welcome; thrust oneself in as if by force
112.	**Invert**	(v.) to turn upside down; to reverse
113.	**Invoke**	(v.) to call upon for support
114.	**Monograph**	(n.) a written account of a single subject
115.	**Persist**	(v.) to refuse to give up; to keep going
116.	**Perspire**	(v.) to sweat
117.	**Persuade**	(v.) to convince
118.	**Pertain**	(v.) to relate or refer to
119.	**Perturb**	(v.) to trouble, make uneasy; to disturb greatly; to throw into confusion
120.	**Pervade**	(v.) to spread throughout
121.	**Precede**	(v.) to come before
122.	**Precept**	(n.) a rule of conduct or action
123.	**Precise**	(adj.) accurate; definite; exact
124.	**Preclude**	(v.) to prevent
125.	**Prefect**	(n.) a chief officer or chief magistrate
126.	**Prescient**	(adj.) having foreknowledge or foresight, being able to see the future
127.	**Prescribe**	(v.) to order as a rule or course to be followed; to order for medical purpose
128.	**Preside**	(v.) to exercise management or control; to occupy a place of authority; to act as the leader over an assembly
129.	**Proactive**	(adj.) serving to prepare for, intervene in, or control an expected occurrence or situation, especially a negative or difficult one; anticipatory
130.	**Proceed**	(v.) to come or follow after

131. **Propel** (v.) to cause to move towards; push

132. **Proscribe** (v.) to outlaw, prohibit, forbid

133. **Prospect** (n.) a formal proposal

134. **Protract** (v.) to draw out or lengthen (in time); to extend

135. **Protrude** (v.) to stick out, thrust forth

136. **Provision** (n.) something supplied as meeting a need

137. **Provoke** (v.) to anger, arouse, bring to action; to stir up

138. **Recede** (v.) to go back

139. **Recite** (v.) to say again

140. **Recluse** (n.) a person who leads a life shut up or withdrawn from the world; someone who lives alone and is separated from the rest of society

141. **Recur** (v.) to happen again

142. **Reform** (v.) to form something again

143. **Remit** (v.) to transmit or send (money, a check, etc.) to a person or place, usually in payment.; to pardon or forgive

144. **Renounce** (v.) to give up or resign something; to abandon or disown

145. **Repel** (v.) to push, drive, or keep away

146. **Repleted** (adj.) filled to satisfaction

147. **Replicate** (v.) to duplicate; to clone or copy

148. **Repose** (v.) to rest; lie; place
(n.) relaxation, peace of mind, calmness

149. **Reprehend** (v.) to criticize, disapprove of

150. **Repress** (v.) to keep or put down; to keep under control or check

151. **Reside** (v.) to live in a particular place

152. **Respiration** (n.) breathing

153. **Restructure** (v.) to build again

154. **Retain** (v.) to hold or keep

155. **Retort** (n.) a quick reply to a question or remark (especially a witty or critical one)
(v.) to respond in such way

156. **Retract** (v.) to take back

157. **Revert** (v.) to return, go back

158. **Revoke** (v.) to make invalid; deactivate; to cancel or withdraw

159. **secede** (v.) to leave or withdraw.

160. **Seclude** (v.) to keep away from others; to isolate

161. **Seduce** (v.) to lead astray from duty or moral conduct; persuade one to do wrong

162. **Segregate** (v.) to separate or isolate from others

163. **Submerge** (v.) fill or cover completely, usually with water

164. **Subsequent** (adj.) coming after or later; following in time, place, or order

165. **Subvert** (v.) to upset; to overthrow; to ruin or destroy

166. **Suppress** (v.) to stop by force, put down

167. **Suspire** (v.) to breath; to sigh

168. **Sustain** (v.) to support, nourish, keep up; to bear up under, withstand; to affirm the validity of

169. **Transcribe** (v.) to make a written copy of; to translate into another language.

170. **Transpire** (v.) to come about, happen, or occur

Prefixes are word parts that create new meaning when they are added to the beginning of a word. Let's take a look at the prefixes "im, il, ir, dis, non, & un."

Word	Meaning
visible	can be seen
responsible	someone that you can trust to do what they should do
literate	someone that can read and write
possible	can be done
polite	having manners and acting properly around others
stop	no more movement
smoker	someone who uses cigarettes
popular	liked by many people
able	having the ability to do something; can do it
honest	tells the truth

Prefix	Word	Write the new word (prefix + word)	New meaning
in	visible	invisible	Can't be seen
ir	responsible		Can't be trusted to do what they should do
il	literate		Can't read and write
im	possible		Can't be done
im	polite		Not mannerly, behaving badly
non	stop		Always moving
non	smoker		Doesn't smoke
un	popular		Not liked by many people
un	able		Lacking the ability; can't do it
dis	honest		doesn't tell the truth

Prefix	Meaning	Examples
In, im, il, ir	not, opposite of	Invisible, impossible, illiterate, irresponsible
dis, non, un	not, opposite of	Dishonest, non-smoker, unpopular
ab	Away from, not	Abstract, absent, abnormal, absolute
ad	To, towards	Adhere, adjacent, adjure, adjoin
anti	against	anti-American, anti-social, anti-bacterial
con	With, together	concentric, concord, converse
de	Down, away, from	Descend, demolish, depart, defend, deport, defrost
en, im, in	In, on, into	Encircle, encourage, endanger, indwelling, import, incarcerate, enrich
epi	Over, upon	Epicenter, epidermis, epicardium
ex	Out, out of	Exodus, expand, exhale, extract, expel, express
fore	Before, in front of	Forecast, forefront, forefathers, foreknowledge
inter	Between, among	Interrupt, interfere, intermission, interview
mis	Bad, wrong	Mislead, misbehave, misunderstand, misguide
mono	one	Monopoly, monotone, monocycle, monarch, monocle
ob	against	Object, obloquy, obstacle
over	Above, beyond	Overuse, overachiever, overconfident, overeducated
pre	before	Preview, preexistent, preowned, predawn
pro	forward, in favor of	Proslavery, pro-American, proceed, progress

Prefix	Meaning	Examples
re	Back, again	Review, reelect, recreate, reassemble, rearrange, reappear
semi	half	Semicircle, semiconscious, semi-automatic
sub	under	Submarine, submit, subterranean, subway
super	above	Superior, supernatural, superpower, superstar
trans	across	Transcontinental, transmit, transport
under	below	Underachiever, undervalue, underage

Prefix & Root Table

prefix/root	definition	Examples
A-, an-	Not, without	abiotic, abysmal, anaerobic
Ab, abs	Away from, off	Absent, abduct, aberration
Ad-, a-, ac-, af-, ag-, al-	At, towards, very	Adhere, accelerate, amass, alleviate
Ambi-, amphi-	Both, around, on both sides of	Ambidextrous, ambiguous, amphibian
Ambula, ambuli	walk	Perambulation, ambulance, ambulatory
amare	love	Amicable, amorous, amiable
Ana-, an-	Up, back, again, upside, down, wrong	anabaptist, analogy, anabolic
ante	before	antebellum
anti	against	Antitrust, antihero, antisocial
anthrop	human	misanthrope, anthropomorphic
Apo-, ap-	From, off, away from	Apologetic, apocryphal, apocalypse
auto	self	Automatic, autocrat, automaton
be	thoroughly, make, cause, seem	Befriend, besiege, bemoan, belabor, belated
bellum	war	Antebellum, belligerent, bellicose
bene	well	Benevolent, beneficial, beneficent
biblio	book	Bibliography, bibliophile
bio	life	Biology, biodiversity, biodegradable
cap, capit	head	Capital, capitulate, captain
cata	Down, against, completely	Catacombs, cataclysm

cede	go	Recession, concede, accede, concession, secede
cept, cap, capt, ceiv, cip	Take, grasp	Accept, receive, captive, recipient, capacity
chron	time	Chronic, chronology, chronicle
circum	around	Circumlocution, circumspect, circumference
Com, con, co-, col-,	together	Community, conversation, compare, connection contract, combine
contra	Against	Contradict, contrast, contraband
cord	heart	Accord, cordial, discord
corpus	body	Corporation, corporeal, corpulent
cracy	Rule or government by	Democracy, autocracy, plutocracy
cred	To believe	Incredible, credence credit
de	Down, from, off, away from, completely, not	Dehydrated, detain, deficit, devalue, deprive, debrief
demos	people	Democracy, demographics, endemic
dia	Through, across, between, apart, throughout	Diagonal, diagnostic, diagram
dicere	To speak	Contradict, edict, predict
dis	Lack of, not, opposite, apart, away	Disrespectful, discrimiation, disreputable
Duce, duct	To lead	Induce, conductor, deduction, reduce
Em, en	in	Entange, embellish
Equi, equ	equal	Equilibrium, equanimity,
epi	Upon, to, over into	Epilogue, epigraph, epilogue

eu	good	Euphemism, euphony, eulogy
exo	outside	Exoskeleton, exotic, exonerate, inexorable
extro	outward	extroverted
Fer	Carry or bear	Conference, transfer, vociferous
fore	Before, first in rank or position	Foreboding, foresee,
form	Shape, form	Deformed, transform, formation
geni	Give birth	Genesis, generation, genetics
Graph, gram	write	Autograph, diagram, biography
greg	Flock, herd	Segregate, congregation, egregious
Homo, hom	same	Homonym, homophone
hyper	Over, excessive	Hyperactive, hypersensitive, hyperextended
hypo	below, less than normal	hypothermia, hypoglycemia
Im, in, il, ir	not	Impossible, incompetent, illegal, irresponsible
inter	Between	Interfere, intervene, interrupt,
intro	inward	Introvert, introduction, introspective
Ject	throw	Reject, dejected, conjecture
logy	Speech or science	Theology, terminology, logistics, illogical
loqui	speak	Loquacious, elocution, soliloquy
magni	Great, large, big	magnificent, magnify, magnate
mal	bad	Malfeasance, malfunction, malignant

manu	hand	Manuscript, emancipate, manacle
Mater, matri	mother	matriarch, maternal
Merge, merse	Dip, plunge	Submerge, emerge, immerse
meta	Changed, different, beyond	Metamorphosis, metaphor
metron	measure	Centimeter, chronometer, metronome
mid	Being in the middle	Midair, midsection, midterm
mis	wrong	Misinterpret, misjudge, misconstrued
miso	hate	Misogynist, misanthrope
Mit, mis, miss	send	Emit, mission, surmise
multi	Many, much	Multitude, multifaceted, multinational
mono	one	Monotonous, monosyllabic, monopoly
neo	new	neonate, neolithic, neo-Nazi
non	Not, lack of	Nonviolent, nonverbal, nonessential, nonexistent
Ob	against, all over, in front of, towards, after, completely	Obsolete, obstinate, obloquy
omni	every	Omnipotent, omniscient, omnipresent
Pater, patri	father	Paternal, patriarch, patronize
pedo	child	Orthopedic, pediatrician, pedagoue
Ped, pedis	foot	pedestal , impediment, centipede, pedometer, pedestrian
per	Thoroughly, through, by means of, on account of	Percent, impervious, pertain, permeate, perspire
peri	Around, near	Perimeter, periscope, peripatetic, periphery

phile, phil	love	Philanthropist, bibliophile
phobe, phobia	fear	Arachnophobia, claustrophobic
phone	Sound, voice	cacophony, dictaphone, euphony, homophone
plic, play, plex, ploy, ply	fold	Complicated, deploy, imply, display, duplex
poly	many	Polytheistic, polygamist, polygon, polygraph
pon, pos, post	Put, place	Postpone, compose, deposition
pre	before	Preexisting, preeminent, precocious, prequel, preconceived
pro	forward	Propose, promote, proactive, Prohibit, protrude, project, prolific, proficient
re	Back, against	Retract, reform, reminisce, resign, restrain, renovate, revise
retro	backwards	Retrospect, retrofit, retrograde
science, scient, sci	science	Conscience, prescient, conscious
scope	Look, consider, examine	Microscope, periscope
scribe, scrip, scriv	write	Prescription, ascribe, transcript, subscribe
se	apart	segregate , seduce, secede
semi	Half, part, partly, partial, twice	Semicircle, semimonthly
semin	Plant, propagate	Inseminate, seminary
sequ	follow	Subsequent, consequence
somni, somn	sleep	Insomnia, somnolent
sopho, sophi	wisdom	Philosopher, sophisticated

sopor	Deep sleep	soporific
spect, spi, spic, spy	look	Retrospect, despicable, conspicuous, perspective
spire	To breathe	Inspire, aspire, perspire
sist, sta, stan, stat	stand	Resist, status
struct	build	Construct, instruction, obstruction
sub, sur, sus, sup, suf, sug, suc	Under, supporting	Subplot, submarine, subsection, surreptitious, suspect, support, suggest, success
super	Above, beyond, highest	Superfluous, superlative, superhuman
sym, syn	same	Synonym, syntax, sympathy, symbiosis
tele	far	Telescope, television, teleport
temp, tempo	time	Temporary, contemporary
tend, tens, tent	stretch	Extension, contend
tain, ten, tin	To hold	Retain, detention, tenacity
terra	land	Territory, extraterrestrial, subterranean
theo	God	Atheism, monotheistic, theology
tract	To pull	Detract, retract, contract
trans	across	Transport, transpire, transcend
under	Below, beneath, too little	Underage, underachiever, underdeveloped
unda	wave	Undulation, inundate
un	not	Unbeatable, unsanitary, unsympathetic, uncaring
uni	one	Unicorn, unicycle, uniform

vac	empty	Vacuum, vacuous, vacant
valer	be stronger or more able, have greater power	prevail
vere, vener	Respect, worship	Venerable
ven, vent, vene	come	prevent, advent
verb	word	Verbatim, verbose, verbal
vert	turn	revert, inverse
volent, volence	will	malevolent, benevolent
voc, vok	to call	vocal, vocation

Suffix Table

Suffixes	Definitions	Example words
-able, -ible	Can be done	Feasible, escapable, indefensible, understandable
-al, -ial	Having the characteristics of	Cordial, beneficial, verbal, structural
-arch, -crat	One who rules	Monarch, autocrat, aristocrat, oligarch
-archy, -cracy	Rule by, type of government	Monarchy, democracy, oligarchy, aristocracy
-ed	Past tense verbs	Aged, etched, ebbed
-en	Made of	Shaken, sunken, broken, wooden
-er	Comparative	Better, fitter, braver
-er	One who	Sitter, usher, voter
-est	Comparative	Kindest, farthest, deepest
-ful	Full of	Grateful, bashful, meaningful
-gram, -graph, -graphy	Writing	Choreography, autograph, telegram
-ic	Having characteristics of	Ethnic, poetic, exotic, heroic
-ing	Verb form/present participle	Quitting, giving, living
-ion, -tin, -ation, -ition	Act, process	Elation, rendition, traction
-ism, -ist	Belief in, practice of, one who believes in	Ventriloquist, racism, misogynist, hinduism
-ity, -ty	State of	Gravity, difficulty, complexity

-ive, -ative, -itive	Adjective form of a noun	Productive, attractive, creative
-less	without	Feckless, hapless, rudderless
-ly	Characteristic of	Willingly, practically, frequenty
-mania	Madness about, passion for	megalomania , kleptomania, egomaniacal
-ment	Action or process	Betterment, ailment, empowerment
-ness	State of, condition of	Newness, madness, illness
-ous, -eous, -ious,	Full of, possessing the qualities of	Gracious, courteous, treasonous
Path, pathy	Feeling, suffering, emotion	sympathy, empathy, apathy
-s, -es	More than one	books, cats, toes, classes
Tics, logy, nomy	Art, science, system, study of, science of	Semantics, astronomy, archaeology
-y	characterized by	Nosy, healthy, risky, bossy

List of color-coded word parts

Purple Cards

Roots/Prefixes	Meaning	Color Number
a-, an	not, without, (having) no	P1
ab, abs	away from, off	P2
ad, a, ac, af, ag, al	at, towards, very	P3
ambi, amphi	both, on both sides of, around	P4
ana, an	up, back, again, upside down, wrong	P5
anti	against, opposed to, opposite of, instead	P6
apo, ap	from, off, away from	P7
be	thoroughly; to make, cause, or seem	P8
cata, cat	down, against, very, bad(ly), completely	P9
com, con, co, col	with, together, completely	P10
de	down, from, off, away from, down to the bottom, totally, completely, not, do the opposite of	P11
dia, di	through, across, between, apart, throughout	P12
dis, di	lack of, not, do the opposite of, apart, away, completely	P13
dys	bad, disordered, difficult	P14
e, ec, ex	out of, from, upwards, completely, deprive of, without, former	P15
el, em, en, im, in	near, at in, on, within, in, into, completely	P16
endo, ento, end, ent	within	P17
epi, ep	upon, to, on, in addition to, against, into, over	P18

eu, ev	good, well	P19
exo, ecto	outside, external	P20
extro	outward	P21
fore	before in time, rank, or position	P22
hyper	over, excessive	P23
hypo, hyp	below, less than normal	P24
in, im, il, ir	not, opposite of	P25
inter	among, between, in the midst or middle of	P26
meta, met	after, changed, different, beyond	P27
mal, male	bad, wrong, ill	P28
mid	being at or near the middle point of	P29
mis	bad, wrong	P30
mono, mona	one, alone; containing one	P31
multi	many, much	P32
non	not, lack of, not at all	P33
ob, of, oc, op, o	against, all over, in front of, to, towards, after, completely	P34
over	beyond, above, upon, in, across, past; on high	P35
poly	many, much	P36
para, par	beside, alongside, related to; disordered, sideways, wrong, contrary to, different (from)	P37
per	through, very, during, by means of, on account of, as in, thoroughly	P38
peri	around, near	P39
pre	before	P40
pro	forward, or in favor of, in front of, before	P41

pros	toward, in addition to	P42
re	back, back to the original place; again, anew, once more, completely	P43
semi	half, part, partly; partial, imperfect; twice	P44
sub, suc, suf, sug, sup, sur, sus	under, supporting	P45
super	above, over, on top (of), beyond, in addition to	P46
syn, sym, syl, sy	with, together, same	P47
trans	across, beyond, to go beyond	P48
un	not, opposite of	P49
under	below or beneath, too little	P50

Yellow Cards

Roots/Prefixes	Meaning	Color Number
equi, equ	equal	Y1
ambi	both	Y2
ambul, ambula, ambuli	to walk	Y3
ami, ama, amic	friend, lover	Y4
amor	to love	Y5
ante	in front of previous, existing beforehand	Y6
anthrop	man	Y7
ation, ion, ition, tion	act of, result of, state of	Y8
auto	self	Y9
bell, bellum	war	Y10
bene	well	Y11
biblio	book	Y12
bio	life	Y13
cept, cap, capt, ceiv, cip	to seize, to take	Y14
cap, capit	head	Y15
cede	to go away, withdraw, give ground	Y16
chron	time	Y17
circum	around, all around, on all sides	Y18
comitari	to join as a companion	Y19
contra	against	Y20
cord	heart	Y21
corp	body	Y22

cracy	rule or government by	Y23
cred	to believe	Y24
demo	people	Y25
dica	to speak	Y26
dict	to say, tell, speak	Y27
duce, duct	to lead	Y28
eu	good, well	Y29
fic, fac, fact, fash	to make or do	Y30

Red Cards

Roots/Prefixes	Meaning	Color Number
fer, lat, lay	to bear or carry	R1
form	to shape, form	R2
ful	full of	R3
gener, geni	to give birth	R4
graph, gram	to write	R5
greg	flock, herd	R6
homo, hom	same	R7
intro	inward	R8
ject	to throw	R9
log, ology	speech or science	R10
less	without	R11
loqu, loqua, loqui, locu, loq, loc	to speak	R12
magni	great, large, big	R13
manu	hand	R14
mater, matri	mother	R15
merge	to plunge, immerse	R16
metron, meter	measure	R17
miso	to hate	R18
mit, mis, miss	to let go, send	R19
multi	many, much	R20

Blue Cards

Roots/Prefixes	Meaning	Color Number
neo	new	B1
omni	all, whole, every kind	B2
ous, eous, ious, cious	full of, characterized by	B3
pater, patri	father	B4
pedo	boy, child	B5
ped, peda, pedis, pedo	foot	B6
per	thoroughly, through, during, by means of, on account of, as in	B7
phile, phil	one that loves, likes, or is attracted	B8
phobe, phobia	fear	B9
phone, phon	sound, voice	B10
plic, play, plex, ploy, ply	to fold, bend, twist, interweave	B11
poly	many, much	B12
pon, pos, post	to put or place	B13
renascence	revival or rebirth	B14
retro	back, backwards	B15
science, scient, sci	to know	B16
scope	to see, look, consider, examine	B17
scribe, scriv, script	to write	B18
se	apart	B19
semin	to plant, propagate	B20

sequ	to follow, come after, follow after, attend, follow naturally	B21
somni, somn	sleep	B22
sopho, sophi	wise, clever	B23
sopor	deep sleep	B24
spect, spi, spic, spy	to look	B25
spire	to breathe	B26
sist, sta, stan, stat	to stand, endure, persist	B27
struct	to build	B28
sub	under, beneath, below, secondary	B29
tele	far, distant	B30

Green Cards

Roots/Prefixes	**Meaning**	**Color Number**
temp, tempo	time	G1
tend, tens, tent	to stretch, spread out	G2
tain, ten, tin	to have or hold	G3
terra	land	G4
theo	God	G5
tract	to pull, draw, drag	G6
transigere	to come to an agreement	G7
unda, undu	wave	G8
uni	one	G9
vac	empty	G10
vere, vener	Stand in awe of, respect, to worship	G11
ven, vent, vene	to come	G12
verb	word	G13
vers, verse, vert	to turn in some direction	G14
vol	will	G15
potens	powerful	G16
durare	to make hard	G17
terminus	end, limit, boundary	G18
servire	to serve	G19
daman	to conquer, tame	G20

White Cards

Roots/Prefixes	Meaning	Color Number
-able, -ible	can be done	W1
-al, -ial, -tal, -ital	having characteristics of	W2
-d, -ed	verb form for past-tense verbs	W3
-en	made of	W4
-er (adjective)	ending for comparing two things	W5
-er (noun)	one who	W6
-est	ending for comparing more than two things	W7
-ful	full of	W8
-ic	having characteristics of	W9
-ing, -ating	verb form for present-participle verbs	W10
-ion, -tion, -ation, -ition	act, process	W11
-ity, -ty	state of	W12
-ive, -ative, -itive	adjective form of a noun	W13
-less	without	W14
-ly	characteristic of	W15

-ment	action or process	W16
-ness	state of, condition of	W17
-ous, -ious, -eous, -uous , -cious, -tious, -rious, -ulous	full of, possessing the quality of	W18
-s, -es	more than one	W19
-y, -cy, -ncy	characterized by	W20
-gram, -graph, -graphy	something written, writing, instrument for writing, art or science of writing	W21
-ism, -ist	belief in, practice of, condition of, one who believes in, one engaged in	W22
-tics, -logy, -nomy	art, science, system, or study of, science of, systematic study of, science of, system of laws governing	W23
-archy, -cracy	rule by, type of government	W24
-arch, -crat	one who rules, one who advocates or practices, rule by	W25
path, pathy	feeling, suffering, emotion; disorder, disease	W26
mania	madness about, passion for, one having a madness or passion for	W27
-nt, -ent, -ant	(adj.) causing or doing something; (n.) one who takes a course of action	W28
-ate	to cause to become	W29
-ory, -tory, -itory	having to do with, characterized by	W30
-ice	quality or state of	W31
-ure	act, result, or process	W32
-lous, -ulous	Inclined to do, habitually engaged in	W33

-ize	to cause or become	W34
-nce, -ance, -ence	action or process	W35
-or	quality, state, or condition	W36
-ile	pertaining to or characteristic of	W37
-it	verb suffix	W38

1. Abdicate (Purple 2, Yellow 26, White 29)
2. Abstain (Purple 2, Green 3)
3. Acceded (Purple 3, Yellow 16, White 3)
4. Accord (Purple 3, Yellow 21)
5. Adamant (Purple 1, Green 20, White 28)
6. Advent (Purple 3, Green 12)
7. Amicable (Yellow 4, White 1)
8. Anachronistic (Purple 5, Yellow 17, White 22, White 9)
9. Anarchy (Purple 1, White 24)
10. Antebellum (Yellow 6, Yellow 10)
11. Antipathy (Purple 6, White 26)
12. Apathetic (Purple 1, White 26, White 9)
13. Aspire (Purple 3, Blue 26)
14. Autocracy (Yellow 9, White 24)
15. Benefactor (Yellow 11, Yellow 30, White 36)
16. Benevolence (Yellow 11, Green 15, White 35)
17. Bibliophile (Yellow 12, Blue 8)
18. Biodiversity (Yellow 13, Purple 13, Green 14, White 12)
19. Chronometers (Yellow 17, Red 17, White 19)
20. Circumlocution (Yellow 18, Red 12, White 11)
21. Circumspect (Yellow 18, Blue 25)
22. Circumvent (Yellow 18, Green 12)
23. Concomitant (Purple 10, Yellow 19, White 28)
24. Concord (Purple 10, Yellow 21)
25. Congenital (Purple 10, Red 4, White 2)
26. Conjectures (Purple 10, Red 9, White 32, White 19)

27. Conspicuous (Purple 10, Blue 25, White 18)
28. Conspired (Purple 10, Blue 26, White 3)
29. Contradict (Yellow 20, Yellow 27)
30. Contravene (Yellow 20, Green 12)
31. Convened (Purple 10, Green 12, White 3)
32. Dejected (Purple 11, Red 9, White 3)
33. Despicable (Purple 11, Blue 25, White 1)
34. Detracted (Purple 11, Green 6, White 3)
35. Divert (Purple 13, Green 14)
36. Discordant (Purple 13, Yellow 21, White 28)
37. Discredit (Purple 13, Yellow 24, White 38)
38. Disinformation (Purple 13, Purple 16, Red 2, White 11)
39. Disseminate (Purple 13, Blue 20, White 29)
40. Distended (Purple 13, Green 2, White 3)
41. Edict (Purple 15, Yellow 27)
42. Egregious (Purple 15, Red 6, White 18)
43. Empathize (Purple 16, White 26, White 34)
44. Euphonious (Yellow 29, Blue 10, White 18)
45. Explicate (Purple 15, Blue 11, White 29)
46. Extroverted (Purple 21, Green 14, White 3)
47. Gregarious (Red 6, White 18)
48. Implicate (Purple 16, Blue 11, White 29)
49. Incompatible (Purple 25, Purple 10, White 26, White 1)
50. Inconceivable (Purple 25, Purple 10, Yellow 14, White 1)

51. Incontrovertible (Purple 25, Yellow 20, Green 14, White 1)
52. Incredulous (Purple 25, Yellow 24, White 18)
53. Insuperable (Purple 25, Purple 46, White 1)
54. Intercepted (Purple 26, Yellow 14, White 3)
55. Interjection (Purple 26, Red 9, White 11)
56. Interminable (Purple 25, Green 18, White 1)
57. Intervene (Purple 26, Green 12)
58. Intransigent (Purple 25, Green 7, White 28)
59. Introspective (Red 8, Blue 25, White 13)
60. Inundated (Purple 16, Green 8, White 29, White 3)
61. Loquacious (Red 12, White 18)
62. Maledictions (Purple 28, Yellow 27, White 11, White 19)
63. Malevolent (Purple 28, Green 15, White 28)
64. Manuscript (Red 14, Blue 18)
65. Misanthropic (Purple 30, Yellow 7, White 9)
66. Misperception (Purple 30, Blue 7, Yellow 14, White 11)
67. Monarchy (Purple 31, White 24)
68. Monotheistic (Purple 31, Green 5, White 22, White 9)
69. Neologisms (Blue 1, Red 10, White 22, White 19)
70. Obdurate (Purple 34, Green 17, White 29)
71. Obloquy (Purple 34, Red 12, White 20)
72. Obsequiousness (Purple 34, Blue 21, White 18, White 17)

73. Omnipotent (Blue 2, Green 16, White 28)
74. Omniscience (Blue 2, Blue 16)
75. Overextended (Purple 35, Purple 15, Green 2, White 3)
76. Pedometers (Blue 6, Red 17, White 19)
77. Perambulate (Purple 38, Yellow 3, White 29)
78. Perceive (Purple 38, Yellow 14)
79. Periscopes (Purple 39, Blue 17, White 19)
80. Perspicacious (Purple 38, Blue 25, White 18)
81. Pertinacious (Purple 38, Green 3, White 18)
82. Philanthropist (Blue 8, Yellow 7, White 22)
83. Polytheism (Purple 36, Green 5, White 22)
84. Precipice (Purple 40, Yellow 14, White 31)
85. Prescient (Purple 40, Blue 16)
86. Projectiles (Purple 41, Red 9, White 37, White 19)
87. Proscribed (Purple 41, Blue 18, White 3)
88. Recede (Purple 43, Yellow 16)
89. Reconstruction (Purple 43, Purple 10, Blue 28, White 11)
90. Redundancy (Purple 43, Green 8, White 20)
91. Retention (Purple 43, Green 3, White 11)
92. Regeneration (Purple 43, Red 4, White 11)
93. Retrospect (Blue 15, Blue 25)
94. Secede (Blue 19, Yellow 16)
95. Seduce (Blue 19, Yellow 28)
96. Segregate (Blue 19, Red 6, White 29)
97. Subjection (Purple 45, Red 9, White 11)

98. Submerged (Purple 45, Red 16, White 3)
99. Subservient (Purple 45, Green 19, White 28)
100. Susceptible (Purple 45, Yellow 14, White 1)
101. Synchronous (Purple 47, Yellow 17, White 18)
102. Tenable (Green 3, White 1)
103. Tenacious (Green 3, Blue 3)
104. Theocracy (Green 5, Yellow 23)
105. Transitory (Purple 48, White 30)
106. Unambiguous (Purple 49, Yellow 2, White 18)
107. Untenable (Purple 49, Green 3, White 1)
108. Venerating (Green 11, White 10)

SPELL WELL
READ WELL
ScholarSkills

Made in the USA
Middletown, DE
23 March 2024